D1480047

PILLOWS
CURTAINS
& MORE

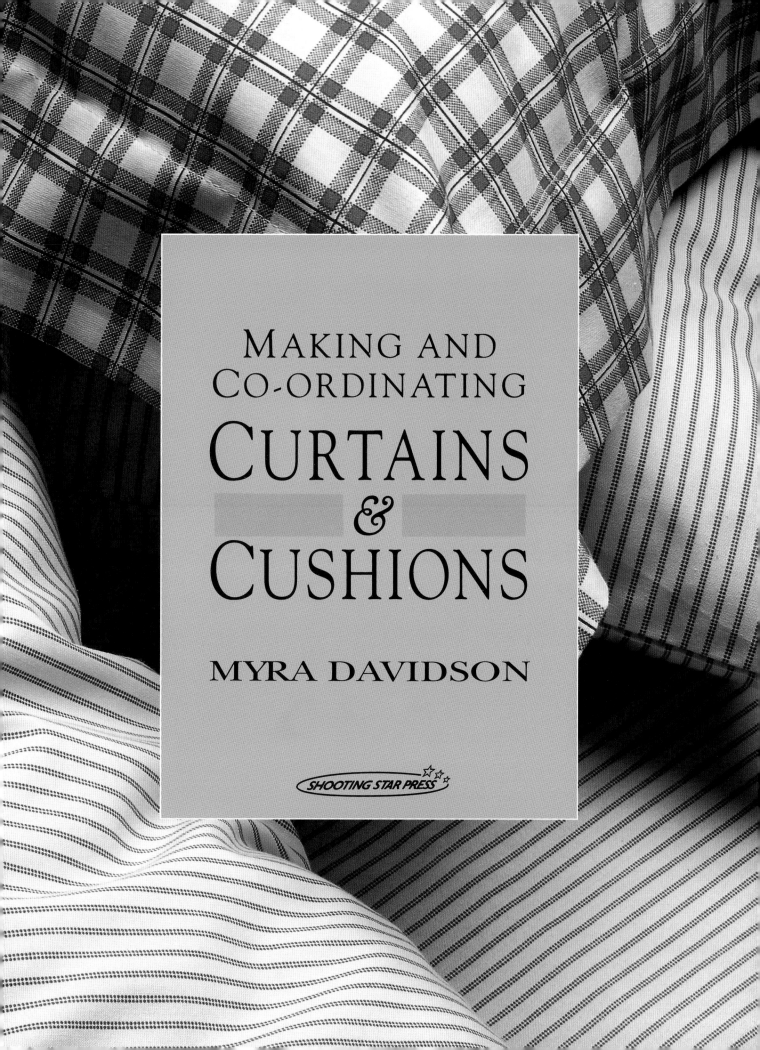

MAKING AND
CO-ORDINATING
CURTAINS
&
CUSHIONS

MYRA DAVIDSON

SHOOTING STAR PRESS

A QUANTUM BOOK

Published by Shooting Star Press, Inc.
230 Fifth Avenue, Suite 1212
New York, NY 10001
USA

Copyright © 1993 Quarto Inc.

This edition printed 1996

ISBN 1-57335-483-X

This book was produced by
Quantum Books Ltd
6 Blundell Street
London N7 9BH

Printed in China by Leefung-Asco Printers Ltd

CONTENTS

SETTING A STYLE

Before choosing colors and materials for soft furnishings for your home, you need to decide on the style you wish to create. This section gives guidance on the considerations to bear in mind when choosing a style that will suit your home, your family and your lifestyle. Advice is given on how to achieve a fully coordinated look as well as practical suggestions on how to create the desired effect.

SETTING A STYLE

CREATING A SUCCESSFUL look by coordinating colors, patterns, and textures is great fun and has endless possibilities, but a mistake can be costly as well as disappointing and can ruin the whole look. To try to avoid this, it is useful to know a little about the basics of interior design – this will help you to make the right sort of judgments when deciding to match or contrast to create a certain look.

The only way to begin is by considering the room you want to decorate. Try to look at it as dispassionately as possible, and consider the amount of natural daylight it receives, its basic size and shape, and the number, shape, and type of windows. See whether there are good features which you may want to enhance, or ugly ones such as radiators, runs of pipes, or large built-in items which you want to disguise.

▲ *Mixing complementary florals and stripes on fabrics and wallcovering gives immediate impact.*

▲ *Pillows and bedding in understated colors soften a minimalist bedroom.*

You will also need to consider the way you use the room, its purpose and function – and your family's requirements. This may restrict your choice of color and surface treatments – there is no point in using pale colors, fragile textures, and flowing drapes in a well-used family room, although you might get away with them in an "adults only" living room or a bedroom.

This is where color, pattern, texture, and fabric will come to your aid. The colors you choose for the window treatments, home furnishings, accents, and accessories will give a room ambience and atmosphere, and help you to produce a specific mood. Color is the first thing you notice about a room.

Pattern and texture set the style and can help create a modern, ethnic, or period flavor. Fabric helps to complete the chosen look and add interest.

CREATING WITH COLOR

▲ *White and neutrals create a calm, restful, mood for a bedroom.*

Basically, there are two types of color: the "cool" or receding ones, which seem to go away from you, and the "warm" or advancing ones, which appear to come toward you. The cool colors are blues, blue-greens, greens, blue-lilacs, and blue-grays. They will create a calm atmosphere and make a space look larger, especially if you use pale shades on the main surfaces. But they can give a room a chilly feel, so are best in sunny rooms. The warm colors are the reds, pinks, oranges yellows, and reddish or pinkish browns.

Neutral colors

There is also the range of "non" colors – the neutrals. The only true neutrals are black, white, and gray, but there is a large variety of what are sometimes called "colored neutrals" – beiges, creams, mushrooms, off-whites, and the natural colors of woods, cane, marble, brick, stone, raw wool, flax, undyed cotton, and so on. They generally act as a link or background in a plan, although they can be used alone to create a restrained and relaxing atmosphere. It is essential to add plenty of variety in texture when using neutral colors.

▲ *Stimulating, contrasting orange and blue are softened with neutral beige.*

▲ *Strong, warm, red accents add interest to a cool, mainly neutral scheme.*

Color accents

One secret of the interior decorator's craft well worth knowing is the introduction of contrasting accent colors into a room plan. If you opt for a mainly pale, cool scheme, or a neutral one, add a few touches of rich, bright, hot colors; if you decide on rich, warm shades, add some sharp, cool contrasts. These accents can be provided by trimmings on curtains, tiebacks and valances; pillows and placemats in the dining-room, and valances and bed throws in the bedroom.

Harmony and contrast

Just as there are two basic types of color, there are two basic types of color scheme – those that rely on harmony, and those that make use of contrast.

A harmonious scheme is one where colors next to each other on a color wheel are used; for example, a room decorated in blues and mauves would be harmonious. Such schemes are usually easy to live with, and can create a warm or cool atmosphere, or be a mixture of both, depending on the section of the color wheel chosen.

▲ *Blue for cool elegance is teamed with sunny yellow to add a warm touch to an evocative Edwardian bathroom.*

▲ *To color match the professional way collect some suitable-sized samples and look at them under day and night lighting.*

Color matching

If you want to get color planning right, tackle color matching in a professional way. This means taking examples of existing items with you when you search for the rest of the scheme. If you have decided on a curtain fabric, for example, take a piece with you when you are choosing the material for contrasting accessories or for paint or wall coverings, to check the exact color. If this is not possible, bring home a paint manufacturer's color card or swatch, and hold it against the existing items. Don't forget to match up to built-in furniture such as kitchen units and countertops.

COLOR PLANNING – A FEW BASIC RULES

• Relate color schemes to the room – consider size, shape, and aspect.

• Use warm colors for an intimate, cozy effect; cool ones for a spacious, elegant look.

• Dress cold rooms mainly in warm colors; warm ones in cool colors.

• Decorate large rooms in strong, rich, or dark warm colors – use some bold pattern.

• Choose light, cool colors to make a small room more spacious – use discreet or small-scale patterns.

• Use neutral colors as a link, or to tone down a too-strong color scheme.

• Introduce sharp color contrasts or accents for emphasis; add warm ones to a cool scheme; cool ones in a warm room; clear, bright ones to a neutral scheme.

• Don't use all light colors, or all dark ones – achieve a balance by mixing light, dark, and medium shades.

• Bright, deep, strong colors as well as bold designs and jazzy patterns look bolder used over a large area. Pale or muted colors and small patterns look quieter, and can fade almost into insignificance when used in bulk.

Contrasting or complementary schemes are created by using colors which are opposites on a color wheel, such as red and green. They are far more exciting than harmonious ones, and can be highly stimulating, especially if fairly strong tones are used. It is better to use different tints and shades of color to create a successful complementary scheme.

Collect samples of the other items which you propose to use in the room and bring them home. If you are trying to judge the effect of a strong color or bold pattern, try to get as large a sample as possible. Make all the pieces into a color or sample board by pinning them to a rigid piece of cardboard and look at them in the room where you propose to use them, first in daylight and then in artificial light – lighting conditions affect colors dramatically – they can look quite different – and you may find that a scheme which looks lovely in daylight doesn't work in artificial light.

PATTERN AND TEXTURE

SUCCESSFUL DECORATING and furnishing schemes do not rely on color alone – patterns used on the various surfaces play an essential part, too. Both add an extra dimension to a scheme and will help you play some visual decorating "tricks."

Patterns

Bold patterns, for example, are like warm colors – they seem to come toward you and thus will be very dominant. They will make a large area seem smaller and more intimate, but if you use them in too small a space, walls will appear to close in. Bold patterns also create a "busy" and stimulating atmosphere – good for halls, family rooms, and children's rooms, but less good for the main surfaces in a room where you want to relax.

Small and mini-print patterns are like cool colors – they seem to pull away from you. They can appear rather bland unless the color scheme is a particularly interesting one, but they are useful for creating an impression of space in a small room. Also use them if you want a relaxing, calm atmosphere.

Size and scale

In order for pattern to work successfully, you need to relate the scale of the pattern to the area over which it is to be used. Bold designs look good at large windows, on unbroken walls, or over big tables where the full impact can be appreciated. If you use them for small windows or wall areas or as pillow covers, the impact of the pattern will be lost. Similarly, small patterns are lost if they are used on large areas, so reserve them for broken-up wall areas and neat, short curtains and shades, and smaller pillows.

If you find choosing a decorating scheme difficult, collect pictures from magazines and catalogues. Or take something you like as a "key" – perhaps a patterned, multi-colored piece of upholstery or curtain fabric – and echo the various colors on the other surfaces in the room. For example, a floral curtain fabric patterned in greens, golds, pinks, and reds on a cream ground can be echoed in pink walls, cream woodwork, green floor, red and gold upholstery piped in green, etc.

If you have several plain surfaces which you want to unify, link them with a patterned item incorporating all the colors. This could be used

◄ *Stripes and checks combine to create a smart tailored look on pillows and curvaceous chair; shaggy fringes edge the pillows to soften the angular shape.*

► *Softly-printed patterns on fabrics and walls rely on textural contrast for impact; glazed chintz emphasizes the quality of the painted woodwork.*

on a main surface or introduced in accessories such as pillows. It could be a patterned valance topping solid-colored drapes, or a fabric border used to trim slipcovers and curtains.

Begin with the main pattern and work up the scheme from there – remember a design looks more "fluid" and interesting when made up into curtains, which are softly draped, and can also seem quite different when pulled back on each side of the window.

Textures

Texture is as important as color and pattern. There are several different types of texture – try to achieve a balance between them just as carefully as when choosing a patterned and solid "mix."

Shiny textures – metals, glass, ceramic tiles, marble, gloss and vinyl silk paint, glazed and silky fabrics – all bounce light back at you. They may make a space seem larger, but they can also look chilly. A room with too many shiny surfaces can be uncomfortable to live in, but some glossy textures are essential for stimulation and contrast.

Rough, shaggy, and soft textures – long and looped-pile carpets, sisal, coir and rush matting, brick and stone, cork, unvarnished wood, coarsely woven fabrics, velvets and wool, and matte and rough-cast

▲ *Natural wood and rough rustic brick-work add warmth to the tiled window area, offset by chintz drapes and sheer light-filtering café curtains.*

▶ *Crunchy lace topping over net sheers screens a classic window while brass poles, marble floor tiles and matt-painted walls emphasize the elegant outline of the wooden chair.*

paints – all absorb light, making the surfaces seem duller, more subtle – or in some cases richer.

They create a calm and more relaxing atmosphere, working like the receding colors and quiet patterns. A room with lots of soft and rough textures can be very comfortable and cozy, but it can also be stifling – again good textural contrast is needed to offset them.

Light-filtering textures – lace, net, cheesecloth, voile, open-weave sheers, slatted and rattan blinds, etc. – all allow the light to pass through while at the same time diffusing it. This gives a fragile, delicate, or ethereal quality, and will make the color look paler or more subtle. They work rather like the neutral colors and can provide a much-needed link between contrasting colors, dominant patterns, rough, soft, and shiny textures – and will often add that essential contrast needed to complete a successful scheme.

▲ *Damask and ticking, flock wall-covering and rich mahogany all create a period flavor, enhanced by matching the pillow and chair seat covers.*

VISUAL TRICKS WITH TEXTURE AND PATTERN

• **To make an area look larger and lighter** – use small patterns; "open" geometric prints, which give a greater impression of space; unifying pattern on wall and windows. Pick shiny light-reflecting textures for walls, ceilings, and woodwork; use sheer fabrics or slatted blinds at the windows; add some shiny metal in furniture or accessories.

• **To make a space seem smaller** – use bold patterns on the main surfaces; contrasting pattern on walls and windows; choose strongly patterned upholstery, bedcovers, and tablecloths to contrast with floor and walls. Select rough, soft, shaggy, and other light-absorbing textures for floor, wall, and window treatments; lots of contrasting effects.

• **To add height to a room** – use strong vertical stripes and patterns for wall and window treatments; bold plain curtains or shades to contrast with the wall.

• **To lower a tall ceiling** – put bold horizontal patterns on the walls in wallcoverings or cladding; use a dado/picture rail/frieze/cornice treatment to create strong horizontal architectural features; use similar patterns, slatted shutters or louvers at windows.

• **To add width to a narrow room** – use bold linear patterns widthwise across the floor. Or use light and dark tiles laid in a checkerboard fashion; select horizontal wall and window treatments as above.

• **To shorten a long room** – use bold patterns on the narrow ends (could be curtains at one end with coordinating wallcovering or a "dress" curtain at the other); break up floor area with defined patterns – a rug or borders going across the room; use contrasting textures – rugs on boards, linoleum, ceramics, or vinyl.

• **To hide ugly features** – use pattern as camouflage – cover all the surfaces with the same bold design; use light-absorbing textures.

• **To emphasize attractive features** – contrast pattern with solid, using a bold pattern against a richly textured plain background; use light-reflecting textures on the feature you want to emphasize.

FABRIC FACTS

BEFORE YOU SET out to choose a fabric, it is essential to consider, as well as the color and pattern, the type of wear it will get, the "handle" or draping quality, the ease of care and cleaning, and the safety factor – whether it is flame-resistant.

Consider the "feel" you want to give a room and choose the fabrics accordingly. If you want a rather grand and formal treatment, then velvets, silks, brocades, and damasks will help to create the look. For a fresh, country scheme, on the other hand, flower patterns and crisp chintzes would be better, or miniprint florals and checked gingham.

If you want a definite period flavor, there are authentic designs available from some manufacturers, some of which may have been re-colored to suit today's furnishing trends. For a feminine bedroom, lace, satin, or eyelet lace would be an interesting choice. In a modern setting, crisp geometric prints on cotton, striped ticking, open-weave sheers, closely woven canvas will all follow the theme.

Practicalities

As always, the purpose and function of the room is also important. Bathroom and kitchen window treatments may have to cope with grease and steam, while curtains, pillows, and slipcovers in family rooms and children's rooms will need to be laundered fairly frequently. Bedroom fabrics can usually be more fragile.

▲ Crisp cotton pleats well for curtain and pelmet.

If the window is exposed to strong sunlight for a large part of the day, you should choose fade-proof fabrics, avoid strong or bright colors, and don't use silk – even carefully lined and interlined, it tends to rot in sunlight. If you live on a busy road use textiles which are thick and grime/noise-absorbing, but also are easy to clean – and use lining and interlining for window treatments in such rooms.

▲ *Strong designs scaled to suit the surfaces harmonize rather than overpower.*

▲ *When choosing one fabric to coordinate a room, ensure it will be suitable for all uses.*

▲ *Perfectly coordinated pattern and plain fabrics on bed, pillow, windows . . .*

Fibers

The fibers used to make fabrics fall into three groups: natural (cotton, linen, silk, wool); man-made, which are natural fibers regenerated and chemically treated (rayon); and synthetic, which are completely chemically derived fibers (acetate, acrylic, nylon, polyester, etc.).

Fabrics made from natural fibers are generally dirt-resistant and clean well, but may shrink and crumple when cleaned. Materials from man-made fibers resist shrinkage and creasing and are less absorbent than natural cloths. Textiles made from synthetics attract dirt and need more frequent washing, which can spoil the texture. Many modern fabrics combine natural and man-made or synthetic fibers, giving some benefits of both.

▲ *Mix and match contrasting fabrics with bow trimmings and tie-backs.*

▲ *The lines of the slatted blinds are echoed by the striped fabric.*

Try before you buy

Once you have reached a decision, check the fabric for any flaws before you leave the store. Make sure the grain of the fabric/printing is straight; if not, you will not be able to tear it along the grain and may make mistakes when cutting lengths. Rub "budget" fabrics to see if a dressing has been applied to give extra body – this will come out at the first washing or cleaning, leaving the fabric limp and insubstantial. If the fabric is to be used for upholstery or slipcovers, ask about fire retardancy, and whether it is (or can be) treated to be stain resistant.

Always insist on buying fabric from the same roll to avoid any color variation – if you have to order fabric, check that it comes from the same roll or batch number: the latter denotes the date of printing – if all the fabric comes from the same printing, the colors should match.

COORDINATION

SUCCESSFUL COORDINATION can be tricky, and if you are a little unsure of how to cope there are plenty of ready-made coordinated or companion collections available which you can see – often in pattern books – at local suppliers.

These can include wallcoverings, borders, and several different fabrics for curtains, upholstery, bed-linens, and sheers. Some lines even extend to waterproof fabric for shower curtains, ceramic tiles, flooring, and accessories. The simpler companion collections have the same pattern printed on (or in some cases woven into) fabrics and wallcoverings. Others may have an identical design, but in a different style, so that you can use a bold print at the window and a smaller version of the same pattern on the upholstery, or combine a strong wall treatment and curtains with a companion miniprint fabric for window shades.

▲ *Checks, stripes and florals in coordinating mode.*

Pick and mix

But you need not be limited by ready-made companion ranges; if you prefer, you can mix and match to suit your own taste. You could experiment with using several lines from one manufacturer to achieve an original yet coordinated look, or select from several sources, since so many makers now work to a similar color palette. Bear in mind, however, that this will only be effective if you choose a similar color theme and similar motifs – for example, all florals, all geometric, or all ethnic designs. These can be in a different scale, depending on the size of the area.

Pillows give you a good opportunity to start pattern mixing. Choose a fabric for the pillow to suit the basic shape – checks and stripes on a square, box, or rectangular shaped pillow; florals for circular and heart-shaped ones – or be bold – try a check pattern on a heart-shaped pillow. Add a ruffle in a different pattern, colored to coordinate. Try contrasting cording on a solid pillow to define the shape; trim with smart checkerboard braid – or lace and eyelet lace if this suits the style. Pile pillows of different shapes, sizes, and patterns on beds, sofas, chairs, and window seats.

▲ *Mini-print patterns and lots of frills are teamed with plain walls.*

▲ *Well thought through coordination – the vase motif is highlighted on the pillows.*

▲ *Range of patterns all from the same color palette.*

This approach can work well at the window, too. A solid or striped valance could combine with floral-patterned curtains, or you could have a shaped plain valance above paisley-patterned curtains over a checked or striped Roman shade. Or a solid half curtain with an elaborate Festoon shade.

For the bedroom, reversible bed throw or duvet covers and matching or contrasting pillowcases can complete the fully coordinated look, while matching placemats and napkins with a contrasting tablecloth make an ideal finishing touch in the dining room.

Personal touches

Coordinating or contrasting fabrics add a personal finishing touch which gives a scheme personality and individuality. If you have enough fabric, make matching accessories such as pillows, napkins, or tiebacks, or add a ruffle or covered buttons to an existing item.

Small pieces can be used for patchwork – if you are using old and new fabrics, try to combine like with like – a similar fiber, weight, and texture, or there could be problems with shrinkage and puckering when the item is washed or cleaned.

A larger piece of leftover curtain fabric can be converted into a throw to hide a less-than-perfect cover on chair or sofa, or add braid, lace,

◄ Pillowcases, pillows, bolsters, duvet and coordinating valance link with frilled pelmet and tailored tie-backs.

COORDINATING TRIMS

• Ties in a matching or contrasting fabric make pretty fasteners for pillows or can be attached to curtains and tied to rods and poles for an attractive heading.

• Add a button covered in a coordinating fabric to a pillow or the base of each curtain heading pleats. pleats.

• Add contrasting tassels to each end of a bolster pillow or to the end of a plain tieback.

eyelet lace or a ruffle as trimming in keeping with the overall color scheme. An even larger remnant can be used to "tie up" a small chair whose cover is past its prime, and wide sheeting or a large bedcover can similarly cheer up a tired sofa and coordinate with new curtains.

Matching or contrasting fabric can also be used to hide the plumbing under a bathroom or bedroom sink and transform it into a vanity unit. You can pleat and head the top to match existing or new curtains and use curtain track, or shirr it onto a curtain wire held in place with hooks

• Use matching or contrasting fabric to make ties for napkins instead of napkin rings.

• Add ruffles to placemats, pillowcases, window shades, tablecloths, and tiebacks in a coordinating fabric to highlight a color accent.

• Contrasting piping can be used to pick out a harmonizing color on pillows, valances, and tiebacks.

screwed to the wall, or use touch-and-close fastener. Dressing tables can be given a similar treatment.

Tailored Roman shades in a dining area can be trimmed with braid to match the paneling on the door or shutters. And if your table is less than beautiful, you could add a floor-length tablecloth in the same fabric with a contrasting or lace over-lay.

CURTAINS

The whole process of making curtains should be a pleasure, from choosing the fabric to the final press; but because of the amount of fabric involved, it can often be a daunting task. Following the guidance in this section, from the measuring of windows to the step-by-step instructions, will enable you to make professional-looking curtains for any room. There are simple unlined curtains made by machine, lined curtains, and interlined and lined ones suitable for more expensive fabric, as well as how to adapt "glass-curtain" fabrics.

Seven steps to successful curtains

The following pages explain in detail the questions you should ask yourself and the considerations you should ponder BEFORE buying fabric. This is a quick checklist to help you to achieve results you will be happy to live with for many years.

1
THE ROOM

Curtains are just one item in a room. If you are lucky enough to be decorating the whole room from top to bottom, it is easier to achieve a truly stunning co‑ordinated look. But, for most of us, it is a question of mixing and matching with what is already there.

Adding accessories in the new curtain fabric can help pull a room together without costing a fortune.

Style
Do you want to change the style and feel of the room? Make it look warmer or cooler? Or are you happy with it as it is?

Enhance or Hide
Are there features in the room that can be brought out or hidden by new curtains?

Practicalities
Who will be using the room and when? Is it important to have easy-to-wash unlined curtains or thick interlined curtains to keep in warmth and keep out light? Are the radiators beneath the windows – in which case heat will be lost if you choose full length curtains.

2
THE WINDOWS

It is important to choose curtains that work well with the shape and size of your windows, both when the curtains are open and closed.

Size and Shape
Do you want to make a window look bigger, smaller, shorter, or taller? Consider your choice of fabric and the positioning of tracks and poles.

Open and Shut
Will your choice of curtain and track make it difficult to open, close, or clean windows or patio doors?

Light and Outlook
Do you want more light in a room for reading or studying? Do you want to block out the sun to avoid fading? Do you want to hide a really ugly view? Consider different types of curtains and/or shades that will help with these problems.

3
CURTAIN ACCESSORIES

Assessing the style of your room and the shape of your windows inevitably extends your thoughts beyond a plain pair of curtains to tie backs, valances, swags, and rods.

Decide Now
It is important to decide, before buying fixtures or fabric, if you want any accessories as it will affect the type of track you buy and the amount of fabric you will need.

Inspiration
Take your time deciding. Look through this book, through magazines, and in the homes of friends and neighbors while thinking of your own room. It is worth thinking hard about as surprisingly little extra effort can turn a pair of homemade curtains into an interior designer's dream.

4 TRACK OR POLE?

It is best to choose your curtain track or pole and your curtain fabric at the same time to make sure the track is suitable to hold the weight of your chosen fabric and that the fixture and the fabric look good together. But DON'T BUY the fabric until the track or pole is on the wall or window. Only then can you take accurate measurements.

What Type?

A wide range of tracks and poles is now available. Look in local stores and browse through magazines for an idea of what's on the market before making expensive decisions. Consider the type of curtain the track or pole is for. Also, do you need to bend the track around curves or bays? Will the track show or be hidden by the style of curtain heading you choose? If it shows will you need to hide it with a valance.

Position with Care

You will need to decide on the position of the track or pole in relation to the window – for example, if you want to pull the curtains right back off the windows, you will need extra length.

5 HEADINGS

Curtain fabric has to be attached to the curtain tracks or poles and this is usually done with heading tape. This tough tape is sewn to the top of the curtain and has pockets in it into which hooks can be slipped.

What Type?

There are many different kinds of heading tape available which give different effects. Consider one that will suit your overall chosen window style, from simple gathers to more formal goblet pleats.

Heading Tape

Your choice of heading tape affects the amount of fabric you will need to buy. More elaborate headings usually require more fabric.

Types Available

Standard gathered tape
Pencil pleat tape
Pinch pleat tape
Box pleat shape
Contact heading tape

6 MEASURING

Only when you have fixed the track or pole in position, chosen the style of heading tape, and decided if you want any matching accessories can you measure accurately and calculate the amount of fabric needed.

Drop

To measure the drop or length of the curtain, measure from the point where the curtain will be suspended to your chosen length. Add allowances for top and bottom hems.

Width

To measure the width, measure the length of the track or pole, adding extra if you have an overlap arm.

Heading

Check the fullness of fabric needed for the heading of your choice and multiply by the track length.

Fabric

Now you must relate these length and width measurements to the width and pattern of the fabric of your choice.

7 BUYING FABRIC

Putting fabric last in this checklist doesn't mean that you shouldn't be thinking about fabric choices from the minute you decide to make new curtains. It just means that you shouldn't BUY any fabric until all the other considerations have been taken into account.

The best thing to do is to bring home swatches and samples of material while you ponder stages one to six. Look at the samples under different lights and at different times of day. Hold them against existing furnishings to judge the effect.

Cost

Big repeating patterns will probably require extra fabric to match the pattern when you join seams.

Color, Texture, and Pattern

Will they harmonize with existing furnishings and give the effect you want?

Practicalities

Will it wash if necessary? Will it need lining to keep out light or keep in warmth?

Extra Fabric

For matching or contrasting accessories like tie backs and valances and for additional items such as bed linen.

MAKING ASSESSMENTS

WHATEVER THE STYLE of home, windows are a natural focal point in a room, and every window has exciting decorative potential. The way you dress your windows is more than just a question of choosing a fabric in keeping with other furnishings in the room and hanging a straightforward pair of curtains. The right treatment can dramatically improve or alter the appearance of even the most uninspiring window and bring character and distinction to the interior of any room.

Curtains are the natural choice for window dressing. Not only do they provide pattern, color, and texture; their value in practical terms cannot be ignored. They provide privacy, and a screen to blot out a grim view if necessary; they can be made so that they block outside light completely or let controlled amounts in; and above all, well-lined curtains are a helpful means of insulation – keeping the warmth in and drafts out. Well-chosen curtains can enhance a feature window or dress up a dull one, and they can visually improve the proportions of an odd-shaped room and transform the outward appearance of the most drab exterior.

Of course, there are no hard and fast rules; your own personal taste is what counts in the final analysis. But don't be rushed into making a decision you may come to regret – remember that fashions come and go, in home furnishings as in anything else, and your final choice is one you are likely to live with for a long time.

▲ *The tie-backs, pelmet and coordinated fabric make the window an attractive focal point.*

Choosing a style

Because curtains can make such an impact on a room, it is vitally important to choose the right style to suit the situation. There is a wide variety of treatments to choose from, but both the style and the fabric should always relate to the size, shape, and architectural style of the window.

For example, large windows which dominate a whole wall in an elegant townhouse demand a lavish dressing with luxurious folds of fabric and decorative headings, but this grand approach would be quite wrong for small attic windows. These need a simple uncluttered treatment, in crisp country fabrics, scaled down to suit an altogether different environment.

Likewise, the window dressing should take into account the way in which the room is used and by whom. Fancy ruffle curtains which might be out of place in a study or in a boy's bedroom could be just right for a feminine bathroom. Expensive fabrics draped extravagantly to the floor might be the perfect touch in a single person's dream home, but could quickly become a nightmare in the family living room.

Practical considerations

Other constraints are often imposed by existing features in the room, such as radiators beneath windows. Here too, personal choice is involved. While it makes the most practical sense to have short curtains that don't restrict the flow of heat into the room, there is no reason why you should not have full-length ones if you wish. In this case, though, it would be best to stick to lighter, more open-weave fabrics and to avoid interlining.

One factor that cannot be ignored, of course, is your budget – even when you make your own curtains, you still have to pay for the fabric, the lining, and the heading tape. As a general rule, most curtains require at least twice the width of a window in fullness, and it is very unwise to skimp on this, as it will only lead to disappointing results. If you need to economize, it is better to opt for a less expensive fabric than to cut down on quantity. Look out for

bargains at sales time or checkout discontinued designs often sold more cheaply by specialist fabric departments. Or you might find that using a solid fabric instead of a patterned one works out cheaper, and you can then invest in more lavish trimmings to bring it into the "designer" class. Draped generously, the cheapest fabric – even lining material – can look good, especially when it has been enhanced with valances or swags and tails.

▲ *Elaborate swags and tails give immediate impact to a window area.*

▲ *Floor draped curtains can look stunning but are not always practical.*

TYPES OF WINDOWS

WHETHER YOU ARE decorating a room from scratch or merely changing the curtains, it pays to take a completely fresh look at your windows, setting aside any preconceived ideas you may have. Sometimes the windows in a house are more or less uniform in size and shape, but often they are not. Where there are several windows of different shapes in the same room, think of the treatment as a whole so that you can create a unifying effect. For a window that is an attractive feature in its own right or looks out on a fine view, consider a treatment that makes the most of its good points. Alternatively, if the outlook is uninspiring and you need a screen from prying eyes, you'll need more than just a simple pair of curtains.

Bay windows

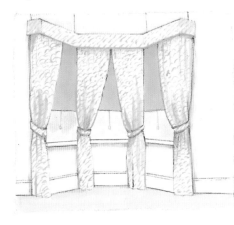

These are always a dominant feature, and curtains need careful planning to avoid costly mistakes. Before deciding on the width and length of the curtains, bear in mind that too much fabric will lead to unsightly bunching at the sides when the curtains are open, whereas too little will look skimpy.

Tall bay windows can take individual pairs of full-length curtains, tied back between the windows and linked with a continuous valance. When the curtains are open, the pair on each side of the central window will make elegant columns of fabric, which will define the angles of the bay.

Where the bay is small or bow-shaped, however, you can treat the window as a single unit, with one pair of curtains, each pulled well back on each side. A way of cutting the cost of curtaining a bay window is to have single-width "dress" curtains (those that are permanently tied back) only at the sides, using shades for each window section to screen them at night.

Picture windows

Horizontal windows

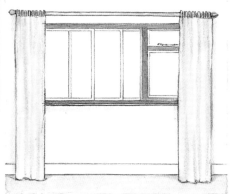

Casement windows

Patio doors and large picture windows, with their vast expanse of glass, can look and feel cold at times, as well as being distinctly bleak at night. Lined and interlined curtains will help with the cold problem; and if they are hung full-length to cover the whole wall, they will make a dramatic focus for the eye. Hang the curtains on a decorative pole or track, allowing enough length for them to be pulled well clear without affecting the opening of the doors. With such a large expanse of fabric, a heavyweight track with a cording mechanism is essential to maintain and protect the appearance of your curtains.

Typical of modern houses, these short, wide windows can be improved with clever dressing to lift them out of the ordinary. Careful positioning of the track or pole, which might be placed higher than usual, can help to correct unsatisfactory proportions. The fabric should be used generously, and preferably full length, except where there is a deep sill or radiator beneath.

These windows are sometimes placed too high to reach easily, in which case permanent sheer glass curtains are often the only solution. Alternatively, if you must have curtains that open, use a track with a cording mechanism, and leave the cords extra long so they can be operated from ground level and wound around a cleat when the curtains are open.

These double windows, usually opening out and hinged on both sides, are common to many houses. If they are deepset, curtains can be mounted on track fixed inside the recess. However, if you prefer floor-length curtains, or those that hang just below the sill, you can fix the track or pole on the wall above the window.

Casement windows are sometimes arranged in groups of two, three, or four, in which case the track or pole can run right along the length.

◄ *An unused patio door lends itself to a wide variety of window treatments that might not be possible with a door that's in constant use.*

Pairs of windows

Whatever form these take – they may be a well-proportioned pair side by side, or they may be unevenly sized, or perhaps even placed on either side of a corner – they are generally best approached as a single unit.

Uneven and corner pairs

When adjacent windows differ in size, you can "fool the eye" by treating them as one. Hang the track or pole across both windows at the highest point, and use full-length curtains to compensate for the irregularities in the depth of the windows.

Two windows placed on the sides of a corner with little space in between can make an eye-catching feature when treated as a single unit. In this case you will need either to use a curtain track which is flexible enough to curve into the corner angle or mount a pair of poles, mitered at right angles and with supporting brackets on each side of the joint as well as at each end.

Identical pairs

Dormer windows

Skylights

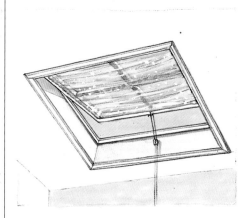

The ideal treatment for two equal-size windows positioned close together on a wall is a pair of full-length curtains headed with a deep valance. If the windows fall short, hang the valance board well above the window to give an illusion of height; if they are narrow, extend the length of the track so that the opened curtains cover the walls at the sides rather than the windows themselves.

For pairs of matching windows with a wide gap between, you can introduce a sense of uniformity by having a third curtain to cover the space during the day. At night, the central curtain can be drawn in both directions to meet the pair on each side, making a feature of a generous expanse of draped fabric.

◀ *Provide balance and harmony between two identical windows by emphasizing the wall space between them.*

Set in an extension projecting from the roof, dormer windows need special treatment, as there is rarely enough room on either side to hang conventional curtains. One solution is to attach a single curtain to the frame itself so that it remains in position when the window is opened. The fabric should obviously be sheer enough to let in the light and is made with cased headings so that the curtain can be suspended from wires stretched across the top and bottom of the frame. Or, use contact tape with the "hook" side attached to the window frame.

Where the dormer recess is especially deep, and the window opens outward, the curtain can be hung from a hinged rod. This will enable it to lie flat against the side wall during the daytime and to be swung inward at night to cover the window. As both sides of the curtain will be visible, you will need to double the amount of fabric and conceal all seams to make it completely reversible.

Many windows at the upper level of the house, or possibly in a new extension, are set into the roof or high up a wall, and some also slope, which adds to the problem of choosing a suitable curtain treatment. One solution is to filter the light, rather than blotting it out completely, by mounting lightweight or sheer curtains directly to the frame on rods, wires, or loop contact and hook tape at the top and bottom, as recommended for dormer windows. In some situations, it may be possible to hang full-length curtains from a pole attached to the ceiling above the window and anchor them in place with a second pole set below the window in the angle where the ceiling and the wall meet.

Sash windows

Old-fashioned sash windows are attractive in their own right and call for a curtain treatment that enhances their elegant proportions. Floor-length curtains look best, mounted outside and above the frame either on tracks or poles, but where there is a deep sill or a radiator beneath, short curtains may be your only option.

▶ *Floor-length curtains are ideal for sash windows and add color to plain walls.*

Arched and round windows

Curtains for arched windows should be designed to emphasize their handsome outline, not disguise it. The simplest option is to hang sill- or floor-length curtains conventionally from a track or pole which is both long enough and high enough to prevent the opened curtains from obscuring the frame in any way.

▶ *Round windows can be stylishly framed with curtains and pelmets.*

Doors and windows

Another potential problem is a glazed door flanked by a pair of small windows. The solution is to hang floor-to-ceiling curtains from an extended length of track so they can be pulled well away to the sides during the day without affecting the opening and closing of the door. If the track is positioned high enough, you could add a plain or ruffled valance along the whole length for a more coordinated look.

TRACKS AND POLES

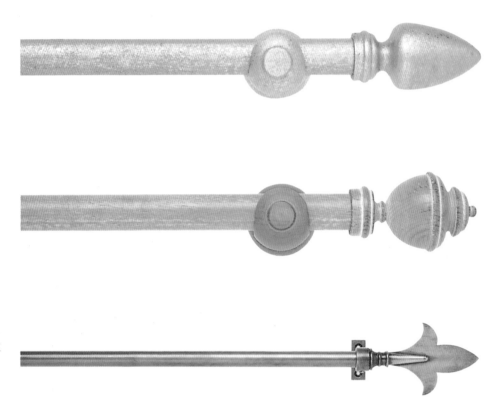

BY THE TIME you have settled on a suitable style for your curtains, you will also have formed an idea of the method by which to hang them. Though the basic choice is between a track or pole, there are so many variations of both that it is worth spending a little time researching the wide choice of options before making up your mind.

Perhaps the most important consideration is whether the type you choose will be strong enough to support the weight of the curtains – many manufacturers produce booklets to advise you, and it makes sense to study them for guidance. Specialist stores and many department stores stock a full – and constantly updated – range of tracks, poles, and accessories, and should have trained members of staff only too willing to share their expertise with you. If they don't, shop elsewhere!

Your preference for a curtain track or pole will largely be determined by the overall appearance of the room. Poles are decorative features in themselves, whereas many curtain tracks are designed to blend insignificantly into the background. For decorative accessories, such as pelmets and valances, you will need to use tracks. A pole is ideal if you prefer the more informal appearance that can be achieved with a swag, when a length of fabric is swathed loosely around it.

In the past, the objection to using a pole was that the curtains could be difficult to open and close, especially at tall windows. However, the introduction of poles with runners and a concealed pull-cord mechanism has considerably increased their efficiency as well as their decorative potential.

CURTAIN TRACKS

IF YOU THINK how often your curtains will be opened and closed during their life span, you will realize how important it is to buy well-made tracks and fittings that will guarantee their smooth running. Most tracks are now made from lightweight, pliable plastic, are cheap to buy and quiet to use, and there are different types suitable for any style of window dressing. "Multi-purpose" tracks are available, but generally it is better to choose a track specifically

designed to take the treatment you have in mind. A basic, inexpensive track is fine for unlined and simple lined curtains, but for large windows and heavy curtains, you will need a sturdier plastic or metal track.

Tracks are usually sold in a standard range of lengths, which can be cut to size, but it is also possible to buy a telescopic type, that allows the track to be adjusted exactly to size as it is being hung. Most curtain tracks are sold in a kit

with all the fittings included, but, if you need to buy them separately, you will generally need one hook and runner per 4 in (10 cm) curtain width, plus one extra for the edge.

As the main purpose of the track is to give support, equal attention should be given to the method of attaching them – some are easier to install than others, but all come complete with full installation instructions. Most, but not all, tracks can be either wall- or ceiling-mounted – check before you buy.

The main types are:

Tracks with gliders

Tracks with gliders (or runners), which slot into grooves on the back of the track, are the ones most generally used for most styles of draw curtains.

◀ *Perfect for swags, café curtains and dress curtains, poles come in all shapes and sizes. Choose one that coordinates with the colors of the curtain fabric and with finials that reflect the overall style of the room.*

Invisible track

Ultra-slim curtain tracks, sometimes called pelmet tracks, can be used in situations where you want the track to be as inconspicuous as possible – perhaps where it is fitted to the underside of a window frame. Suitable for lightweight curtains, they can be wall or ceiling mounted and can be curved around a bay window.

Visible track

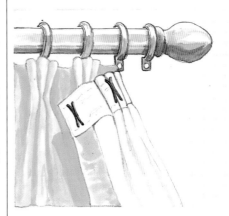

If the track will be in view, that is, not covered by a valance, choose one that is unobtrusive or can be decorated to match your room scheme, either with paint, wallpaper, or fabric. Alternatively, choose a decorative track, say with a gold, silver, or brass finish, and complete with matching finials, that fits in with your style of curtaining and complements your decor.

Bay window track

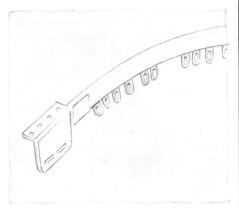

For bay windows, you will need a track that is pliable enough to be bent to fit around the curve – this is possible with most plastic tracks. If the track is warm, it will be easier to bend, so it is helpful to have it at room temperature before you start. However, some are slightly more rigid than others and cannot, therefore, be curved as tightly, so may not be suitable for a right-angled bay – check the manufacturer's literature for guidance on the most suitable choice.

For long and very heavy curtains, you will need a metal track that is strong enough to take their weight. Most metal tracks available can also be bent by hand, but a few – generally those used by professional designers – have to be "made to measure" by the supplier.

Cording and overlaps

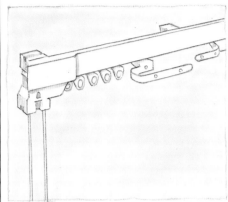

When you are carrying a wide expanse of fabric across a bay or other large window, or where curtains are difficult to reach, it makes sense to invest in a track with an integral traverse system. Supplied ready-assembled, with all the cords in position, and overlap arms where the curtains meet in the center of the window, these tracks help to improve their "hang", maintain their shape, and protect them from everyday wear and tear. As the curtains overlap, rather than butt together, it is important to allow a little extra width in your calculations for fabric.

Though these tracks are more expensive, it is worth the extra cost, especially for delicate or pile fabrics which would be damaged with constant handling. However, certain traverse tracks are only suitable for straight runs – remember to check before you buy.

It is possible to buy a traverse system for an existing track, which includes clip-on overlap arms, but these are generally less efficient than the pre-strung type.

Double valance tracks

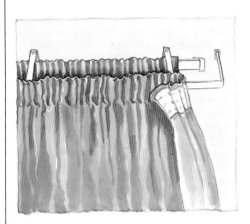

With the revival of the valance as a decorative top treatment for curtains, double tracks with combined valance rails are now widely available. The rail is attached to the track with extension brackets and comes with clip-on hooks which allow the valance to be held firmly in place, but also easy to remove for cleaning. You can, of course, keep an existing track and suspend a shelf above it to take the valance.

▶ *For a bay window choose a pliable curtain track that bends to fit the curve.*
▶ *For a recessed window (far right), a fixed curtain on either side within the recess eliminates the need for a pliable track.*

Glass curtain tracks

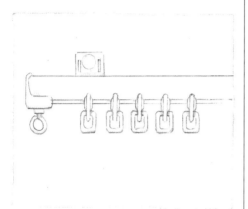

For sheer glass curtains on their own, you can choose from a basic coated sprung wire, special lightweight track, or slimline tension rods which carry the curtains neatly without the need for supporting brackets; used within a window frame, they spring out to grip the sides.

Multilayered tracks

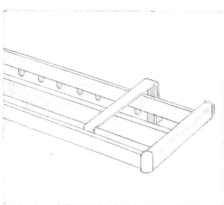

If you are considering a "multilayered" window treatment, with curtains, valance, and glass curtains, for example, it is possible to buy a three- or four-tier system which has separate tracks for each one combined within one unit.

Curtain draw rods

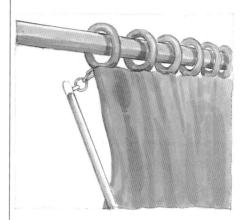

In the absence of a traverse system, an alternative is to attach pull rods to the lead runners at the center of the window and use these to open and close the curtains. Made from wood or metal, the rods are hidden behind the edge of the curtain.

CURTAIN POLES

WHERE A CURTAIN pole is more appropriate for your style of decor, there is a wide variety of sizes and styles to choose from. They are available either in a wood – natural, stained, polished, or painted – or metal finish, such as brass, iron, or steel, and are usually supplied with wall mounting brackets and an appropriate number of rings for the length purchased. (For curtains with a cased heading or rod pocket, you will obviously have no need for the rings). Finials complete the decorative effect of curtain poles – designs range from simple round knobs to fancy acorns, pineapples, and fleurs-de-lis.

Standard curtain pole brackets allow the curtains to project up to 3½ in (9 cm) from the wall, a useful factor where clearance is needed for a radiator or window sill. However, short-reach brackets are also available, as are recess brackets, which allow a pole to be suspended inside a window frame without finials. It is vital to use the right number of brackets for the length of pole – too few, and you risk its bending beneath the weight of the curtains.

Standard poles

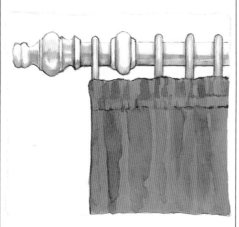

Poles are available in a variety of widths – the choice of diameter ranges between 1 in (25 mm) and 1⅜ in (35 mm), and should be governed by the weight of the curtains the pole has to support. A choice of lengths is also available – if you cannot find the precise size you need, all except solid brass poles can be cut to length and some incorporate a telescope mechanism that allows the pole to be adjusted exactly to size as it is being hung.

Poles are no longer limited to straight runs alone, as it is possible to buy corner connections to bring together two poles for curtaining windows on each side of a corner.

Mini-poles

Designed specifically for café curtains, mini café rods have a diameter between ½ in (12 mm) and ¾ in (19 mm). Sold in either brass or polished wood, they come with rings or clips which grip the top of the curtain, eliminating the need for curtain hooks.

Rod pocket poles

Standard poles can be used for curtaining with tunnelled or pocket headings, where the fabric is simply fed along the pole to create a ruched effect. In this way you can create elegant valances, static curtains, and even swags and tails, quickly and easily.

Traverse poles

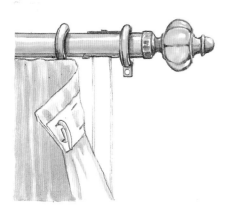

Where it is important to have a cord mechanism for pulling your curtains, traverse rods or poles have a similar appearance to the traditional style, but are fitted with half-rings – for decorative purposes only – and runners concealed at the back. As these tracks are expandable, they offer greater scope for hanging a particularly wide expanse of curtaining.

Traverse poles can be used in conjunction with curtain tracks when a multilayer effect is required.

▶ *Match a curtain with a loop heading to a pole that coordinates with the wallpaper and contrasts with the curtain fabric.*

POSITIONING

WHEN BUYING a pole or track, remember to allow for the extra length required to allow curtains to be pulled back, well away from the sides of the window, to let in the maximum daylight. The distance will depend on the fullness and fabric used, but, if possible, tracks and poles need to extend beyond the window's edge by between 8 and 18 in (20 and 45 cm).

When deciding where to position the track, bear in mind the points made in "Making Assessments" – if it is desirable to improve proportions, for example, raising or lowering the height of the track can considerably affect the appearance of a window that is either too short or too tall.

The fixture should be in position before you measure for your fabric.

Wall above window

The usual position for hanging the curtain track or pole is on the wall above the window, and the ease with which this can be done depends on whether or not there is a concrete lintel above the window which would be difficult to penetrate. One solution is to put up a wooden batten to take the system, but remember it will project out slightly and will be visible when the curtains are open. If you're using a track, it is possible to put a screw eye into the end of the batten close to the wall, so that you can attach the last curtain hook to it to conceal the return.

Window meets ceiling

Where the top of the window meets the ceiling, you have no option but to use curtain track that is suitable for top-hanging, or a pole with specially adapted brackets that means it can be attached to the ceiling. Take extra care when securing the fixture to the ceiling, especially where heavyweight curtains are involved. It is essential the screws are inserted securely. Use anchors or toggle bolts if necessary

HANGING THE TRACK OR POLE
The fasteners for hanging your chosen track or pole will vary from one manufacturer to another, so you should follow the instructions that accompany the system you have bought.

Recessed window

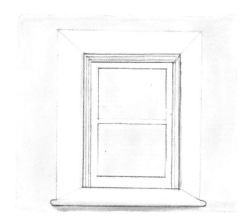

Where a window has a deep recess, you may choose to hang a top-mounted track, or a pole with recess brackets inside it. Here, too, you may come up against the problem of drilling into concrete and would, therefore, have to resort to using a batten.

Window frame

For curtains which need to lie close to the window, sheers for example, a lightweight fixture can be safely attached to the frame itself; but with all other tracks, this position is not recommended as you run the risk of damaging the wood with the screws.

▲ *Poles are stylish heading features for curtains hung above the window.*

▲ *Curtains hung from the ceiling make the ultimate frame for a window.*

HEADINGS

BEFORE ESTIMATING and buying your curtain fabric, you need to decide on the heading style – there is now a wide variety of commercial tapes available, producing decorative effects that range from simple gathers to formal box pleats, and even smocking. Your choice will depend on the effect you want to achieve and, to some extent, your budget. Some curtain heading tapes require more fullness of fabric than others, and it is therefore vital to choose your heading before buying your curtain fabric.

Standard pleater tapes are strips of tough, closely woven fabric, generally in white or cream, sold by the yard. They have pockets for the curtain hooks which attach the curtains to the gliders on the track, making them easy to remove for washing or dry cleaning. For fixed curtains and valances, there are "contact" tapes, which work on the "touch-and-close" principle and require no hooks or rings.

With most pleater tapes, drawstrings running through the tape enable gathers or pleats to be formed automatically as they are pulled up to the fullness required. Alternatively, there is a special tape for pinch and box pleats, where hooks rather than drawstrings, are used to produce a crisp professional-looking heading.

Some of the deeper pleater tapes have more than one row of pockets, enabling you to adjust the height of the curtain according to which row you use for the hooks. With a pole the top row of pockets would be used for the hooks, to allow the pole to be seen, whereas with a track, the hooks go into the bottom row to hide the track when the curtains are shut.

Before estimating your fabric needs, it is necessary to decide which row of pockets will be used for the hooks and include this in your calculations. The top hem allowance will be greater if you are using the bottom row of pockets than if you use the top row. The depth of heading above the hook pocket plus a turning allowance at the top is needed.

Most curtain fabric suppliers should have a wide variety of tapes to choose from, and should also be able to offer you advice and a selection of leaflets produced by different manufacturers giving helpful guidance on using their own specific products. Be sure to refer to these before proceeding to calculate the amount of fabric required.

◀ *Buttons covered in a coordinating or matching material add an eye-catching detail to many items and can be stitched to the bottom of goblet and other pleats for that special touch.*

Standard gathered tape

Suitable for use with lightweight curtains hanging from a track, or those where the heading will be hidden by a valance, the cheapest standard tape is approximately 1 in (2.5 cm) wide. It is generally positioned with a narrow margin of fabric between the top of the tape and the top of the curtain to form a neat ruffle when the cords are pulled up. Where a wider ruffle is required, the use of iron-on stiffening will prevent it from flopping forward, and this is also a good idea to give a little extra body to the heading of sheer fabrics.
• Hook pocket rows: 1
• Fabric fullness required:
$1\frac{1}{2}$ to $2 \times$ the track length
• Clearance from top of tape to top of curtain: 1 in (2.5 cm)

◀ *Elegant triple pleat heading with pole and rings.*

Pencil-pleat tape

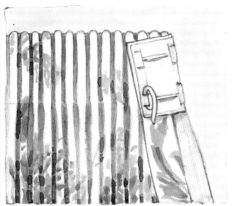

A versatile heading, which suits most types of curtains, pencil-pleat tape is available in a variety of widths and produces uniform, evenly spaced pleats when the cords are pulled shut. Standard pencil-pleat tape can be used with any type of track or pole; the fabric fullness required will depend on the type of fabric used – the thinner the fabric, the more fullness is needed. There is also a mini pencil-pleat tape suitable for lightweight fabrics and a special one for sheers.
• Hook pocket rows: 3 (standard); 1 (mini)
• Fabric fullness required:
$2\frac{1}{4}$ to $2\frac{1}{2} \times$ the track length
• Clearance from top of tape to top of curtain: $\frac{1}{8}$ in (3 mm)

Triple or pinch-pleat tape

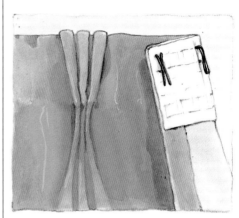

This type of pleater tape produces regular groups of fanned pleats with spaces in between. The pleats are formed automatically by pulling up the cords and inserting special hooks to hold them firmly in place. Stiffer than some tapes, it creates a tall and elegant heading that is particularly attractive with formal lined curtains, and is equally suited to cottons and medium- to heavy-weight fabrics.

As the pleat and space positions are predetermined and cannot be altered, careful placing of the tape is necessary to guarantee that the heading matches across the curtains to give a continuous effect when they are closed. Where a pair of curtains will butt together, always begin by placing the pleater tape at the curtain edge which will lie in the center of the window, starting in the middle of a pleat group, so you will be left with a half space at each edge. With an overlap arm, one complete space on each curtain should be adequate.
• Hook pocket rows: 2
• Fabric fullness required:
$2 \times$ the track length
• Clearance from top of tape to top of curtain: $\frac{1}{8}$ in (3 mm)

Box-pleat tape

Suitable for all types of curtains, particularly heavy, lined ones, box-pleat tape pulls up the fabric into regular neat folds. It is well suited to permanently open "dress" curtains or those teamed with a valance – the top row of hook pockets could be used for the valance, the bottom row for the curtains.
• Hook pocket rows: 2
• Fabric fullness required: 3 × the track length
• Clearance from top of tape to top of curtain: $\frac{1}{8}$ in (3 mm)

Uncorded triple-pleat tape

A deep pleater tape with long narrow pockets running at regular intervals along the full depth, with an opening at the bottom. Instead of drawstrings, long-pronged pleater hooks are used to pull up the pleats – by inserting the prongs into the pockets, you can make single, double, or triple pleats. With this tape, your curtain can be tailor-made to the exact length of your particular system, as you can adjust the amount of fabric in each pleat and the spaces in between.

When using this tape, it is important to work out the approximate width down to which the fabric will pleat, and you should follow the manufacturer's instructions for guidance. A good tip is to pleat the tape before applying it to the curtain, and hook it onto the track or pole to judge the effect. Place the first hook to make a single pleat at each end of the curtain and space the remainder evenly across the width, keeping the design continuous at the center of a pair (see above).
• No. of pockets: (see above)
• Fabric fullness required:
$2\frac{1}{4}$ to $2\frac{1}{2}$ × the track length
• Clearance from top of tape to top of curtain: $\frac{1}{8}$ in (3 mm)

Cartridge or goblet pleat tape

A deep – up to $3\frac{1}{2}$ in (9 cm) – tape which produces cylindrical tubes when drawn up and is especially suitable for heavy, lined, floor-length curtains. As the curtains fall in regular folds, rather than gathers, it is a good choice where a valance is being used. Special hooks secure the pleats firmly in position, and the addition of a little batting or tissue in the opening in the pleats enhances their firm, rounded shape.

Goblet-shaped pleats can be made using the same tape (though a special goblet pleater tape is now available), but by pinching in each pleat at its base with a few hand stitches.
• Hook pocket rows: 2
• Fabric fullness required:
2 × the track length
• Clearance from top of tape to top of curtain: $\frac{1}{8}$ in (3 mm)

Contact heading tape

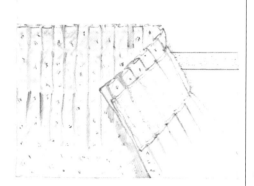

Heading tapes with a contact backing can be used for simpler hanging of gathered valances, lightweight sheers, and curtains at unusually shaped windows. Similar in appearance to conventional tape, with cords which pull up to form the gathers in the normal way, they have a "loop" backing which will adhere to a "hook" tape attached to the curtain track, batten or, in the case of sheers, the window frame. The hook side of these tapes is self-adhesive.

• Fabric fullness required: 2 to 3 × the track length (depending on tape used and application)

• Clearance from top of tape to top of curtain: $\frac{1}{8}$ in (3 mm)

▶ *Attractive rod pocket headings are easy to make and are perfect for dress curtains that remain in a fixed position.*

Rod pocket heading

One of the simplest curtain headings requires no tape, hooks, or rings – a casing or "pocket" is stitched through a double thickness of fabric below the top of the curtain, and a rod, pole, or wire is inserted into it. The fabric fullness is then gathered up, creating a ruffle above it if desired. The fullness needed for this type of heading will vary considerably according to the weight of fabric – the thinner the fabric, the greater the fullness of the finished curtain.

Curtains finished in this way cannot be opened, but they can be looped back attractively on each side of the window with matching tiebacks, or draped over brass or wooden hold-backs screwed to the window frame. This is an ideal heading for valances which always remain permanently in place.

• Fabric fullness required: $1\frac{1}{2}$ to 3 × the rod length (depending on the thickness of fabric)

WHEN YOU ARE ready to position your heading tape, refer to the manufacturer's instructions for the precise amount of fabric clearance between the top of the tape and the top of the curtain for the particular type you are using. There may be some variation, ranging from a mere $\frac{1}{8}$ in (3 mm) for deep heading tapes to 1 in (2.5 cm) or more, for standard gathered tape where a ruffle above it is required. Be sure to include any hem allowances when you are estimating fabric quantities.

1 Cut a length of heading tape to the width of the curtain, adding an allowance of $1\frac{1}{2}$ in (3 cm) for the end turnings. When using drawstring tape, loosen the cords at the end of the tape which will come on the inside edge of the curtain, and knot each one on the wrong side, $\frac{5}{8}$ in (1.5 cm) away from the cut edge. Leave the cords free for gathering at the outside edge by pulling them from the front of the tape and knotting the ends.

2 Turn under the $\frac{5}{8}$ in (1.5 cm) allowance at each end and pin, then baste, the tape in place. Machine stitch first the top, then the bottom, edge of the tape, working in the same direction on each side to prevent puckering. Machine stitch across each end of the tape.

3 To gather a curtain with drawstring tape, hold the free cords in one hand and push the heading along the cords until the fabric is gathered to the width required. Distribute the fullness evenly along the curtain; then knot the cords together on the outside edge. Insert hooks at approximately 3 in (8 cm) intervals along the curtain.

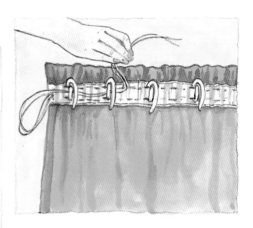

4 Do not cut loose cords of drawstring tape; so they can easily be released for washing or drycleaning. Either thread them through the hooks at the back of the curtain for a short way, or wind them around a cord cleat, which can be hidden behind the outside edge of the curtain.

*Tracks, poles and heading tape
need to be carefully chosen to ensure
you achieve the effect you want.*

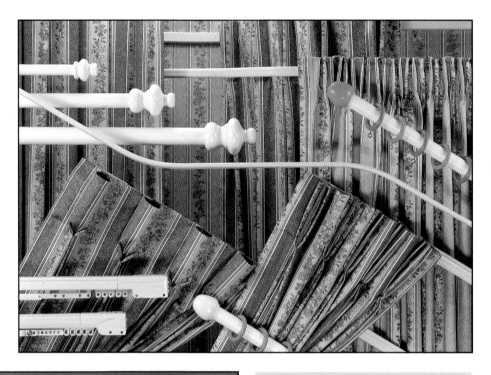

PLEATING

To pleat a curtain with drawstring tape, proceed as above, taking care to avoid puckering between pleats. Hold the top of the curtain firmly in one hand, with your thumb just in front of the first pleat group, and the loose cords in the other. Push the first pleat into position and then move on to the second. Now return to the first, as this will no longer be pleated and continue working back and forth in this way along the curtain until the entire heading is pleated. Knot the cords and insert hooks, if using, into the two adjacent pockets on each side of a pleat to hold it firmly in place.

To pleat a curtain with uncorded tape, plan the position of the pleats, spacing them evenly along the curtain, and insert pleater hooks according to the manufacturer's instructions.

MEASURING THE FABRIC

ONCE YOU HAVE decided on a style of heading for your curtains and hung the track or pole in its desired position, you are ready to estimate the amount of fabric required.

Only two measurements are necessary when making curtains – the drop for the finished curtain measured from the hook suspension point on the track and the length of the curtain track, plus overlap arm if the traverse method of pulling is being used.

Use a steel tapemeasure or wooden yardstick for accuracy and make a note of the appropriate measurements on a diagram of your window, as shown.

A true conversion from metric to imperial cannot always be made, so work following one or the other throughout a project.

TO CALCULATE THE DROP

To calculate the finished drop of your curtains, first you need to decide where they will finish: to the sill, to just below the sill, or to the floor.

▲ **Sill-length** curtains should actually end $\frac{5}{8}$ to $\frac{3}{4}$ in (1.5 to 2 cm) above a protruding sill to give clearance.

▲ **Below-the-sill** curtains should hang below the sill by 2 to 4 in (5 to 10 cm). However, if there is a radiator immediately below the window, end the curtains $\frac{5}{8}$ to $\frac{3}{4}$ in (1.5 to 2 cm) above it.

▲ **In a recess** curtains should end $\frac{5}{8}$ to $\frac{3}{4}$ in (1.5 to 2 cm) above the sill to give clearance.

▲ **Floor-length** curtains require a clearance of 1 in (2.5 cm) if you want to protect the hemline. However, you may choose to make them too long, so the fabric falls in swathes on the floor. If so, remember to adjust your measurements accordingly before starting to calculate for fabric requirements.

To measure the drop

Measure from the point where your curtain will be suspended to your chosen drop.

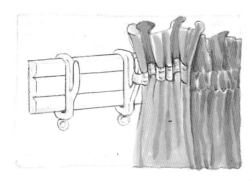

For a pole, this will be the finished drop measurement.

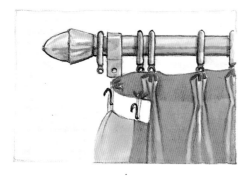

When using a track, rod, or wire, you will need to add the additional depth of fabric from the suspension point to the top of the curtain.

Adding hems

To this finished drop measurement, you need to add the appropriate allowance for the hems at the top and bottom of the curtain, to give you the actual cutting length.

Bottom hem allowance

Unlined	3 in (8 cm)
Café curtains	not appropriate
Rod pocket	3 in (8 cm)
Tube-lined	4 in (10 cm)
Locked-in lining	6 in (15 cm)
Locked-in lining and interlining	4 in (10 cm)
Detachable lining	not appropriate

Top hem allowance

The amount of extra fabric you need to allow for the top hem of your curtain depends on the type of heading tape you choose. For example, the top hem allowance for an unlined curtain using standard tape is 3 in (7.5 cm) to give a 1 in (2.5 cm) ruffle effect above the heading tape.

For the lined curtains, measure from the row of hook pockets being used to the top of the heading tape, then add the following measurements:

Café curtains	not appropriate
Rod pocket	check circumference of pole
Tube-lined	3 in (7.5 cm)
Locked-in lining	⅝ in (1.5 cm)
Locked-in lining and interlining	3 in (7.5 cm)
Detachable	not appropriate

TO MEASURE THE WIDTH

Once you have the drop measurement, calculate the width required. When you have these two measurements turn to the next page to estimate how much fabric you will need.

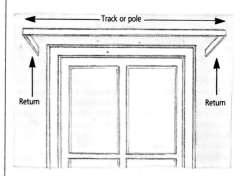

- Measure the length of your track or pole to calculate the width of the curtains when gathered. Add extra for an overlap arm and for the returns at the side.

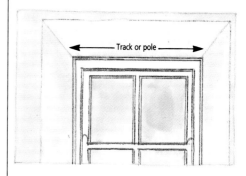

- For curtains that will hang close to the window, measure the actual width of the recess.

TO ESTIMATE FABRIC AMOUNTS

CHECK THE FULLNESS of fabric required for your chosen heading tape (see page 48). This can range from 1½ times to 3 times the actual length of your track or pole.

• Check the width that your chosen fabric is sold in.

• When working with patterned fabrics, especially where the design is large and distinct, think about where the hemline will fall, aiming to avoid an unsightly cut through a whole motif. Bearing in mind that the fullness of the curtain will obscure the pattern, consider the finished appearance at the top of the curtain, too, taking into account where the hooks will be placed in the heading tape for your chosen method of hanging.

• Remember, if you want to make coordinating items buy extra fabric when buying your main curtain fabric.

• See Working with Fabric, page 138.

FOUR EASY STAGES

Multiply the track or pole length by the fullness needed for your chosen type of heading tape, then divide this figure by the width of the fabric, rounding up to the nearest whole number. This gives you the number of widths you will need.

Usually the same track or pole will be carrying two curtains – one for each side – so you need to halve this amount to find out the number of widths in each curtain. If this means you have to divide widths in half, join the half-widths to the outside edge of each curtain.

Once you have established the total number of widths needed to cover the window, multiply this figure by the cutting length to give your total fabric requirement. It is advisable to allow a little extra fabric to enable you to straighten cut edges, and to make any fine adjustments to the finished length.

When using patterned fabric, you will need to make extra allowance for matching – as a general rule, allow one full pattern repeat for each width after the first. Any wasted fabric can be used to make tie-backs and matching pillows.

CUTTING TIPS FOR CURTAINS

• To prepare fabric for cutting, press out any creases. If there is a centre fold this will require a damp cloth and a warm/hot iron to press it out completely.

• Ideally a large table is best for preparing and cutting out fabric. If this is not possible, use the floor.

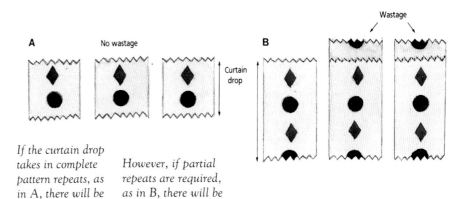

If the curtain drop takes in complete pattern repeats, as in A, there will be no wastage.

However, if partial repeats are required, as in B, there will be some wastage.

LINING

ESTIMATING FABRIC

To calculate for plain fabric for curtains hanging outside the window and reaching the floor. The chosen fabric width is 137 cm (54 in) wide.

		cm	in
1	Measure track length	127	50
	(**A** to **B**)		
	overlap arm	+15	6
	returns	+20	8
2	For pencil pleat heading tape, fabric required is 2.5 times the track length		
	=	405	160
3	Divide this by fabric width, say 137 cm (54 in), (round up to the nearest full width)		
	widths	**3**	**3**

This will make two curtains with a width and a half each,

		cm	in
4	For length, measure	215.5	85
	A to C		
5	Deduct for clearance	2.5	1
	=	213	84
6	Add for hems and heading	2.5 cm	10 in
7	Multiply by required number of widths (3)	238	94
	Purchase:	**7.3 metres**	**8 yards**

This allows a little extra fabric to enable you to straighten the cut edges, and to make any fine adjustments to the finished length

GENERALLY, THE AMOUNT of lining required will be the same as the quantity of the curtain fabric and, as it is plain, you do not require extra for matching. But, as linings are made slightly smaller than the curtains, so you can purchase a little less for each drop required. The width is only reduced by trimming off a margin from the outer side edges, not from each width.

Tube-lined
Cut lining 6 in (15 cm) less each length.
Trim lining 2 in (5 cm) from each outer edge.

Locked-in lining
Cut lining $3\frac{1}{2}$ in (9 cm) less each length.
Trim lining $1\frac{1}{2}$ in (4 cm) from each outer edge.

Locked-in interlining and lining
Cut lining 4 in (10 cm) less each length.
Trim lining 2 in (5 cm) from each outer edge.
Cut interlining as the curtain, after joining widths minus all hems.

Detachable lining
Measure from bottom of existing heading tape to the hem. Deduct 1 in (2.5 cm) and add 3 in (8 cm). Lining can be same width as curtain or $1\frac{1}{2}$ times the track.

DRAPING

Even the most professionally made curtains will not look their best unless they are draped correctly.

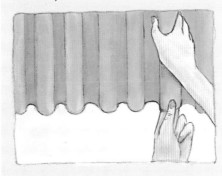

Hold the bottom hem at a position in line with the pleat at the top and gently tug at the hem. Now run your fingers down the length of the curtain along the naturally created folds.

If the curtains hang below the track, push each space between the pleats backwards whilst gently moving the curtains to the side of the window. If the curtain heading covers the track, the spaces between the pleats must be pulled forward, so they stand proud of the track. The draping should be held gently in position at intervals down the length of the curtain, using something soft, such as spare material. Leave at least overnight in order to "train" the pleats.

UNLINED CURTAINS

Unlined curtains are easy to make. They are best for a room such as kitchen or bathroom, where curtains need frequent laundering, and for windows where short curtains are required. Cotton or a polyester/cotton mix is best for a kitchen, and towelling for a bathroom as this withstands a steamy atmosphere.

1 Lay the fabric right side down and turn in each side edge ⅝ in (1.5 cm) to the wrong side. Pin near the cut edge, and press the folds. (If using terrycloth, do not press.)

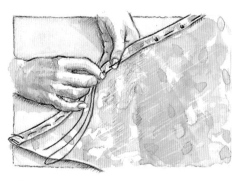

2 Turn in a further ⅝ in (1.5 cm) down each side to form double hems. Pin, baste, and remove the pins. Press the hems.

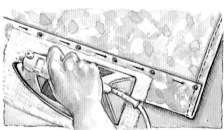

3 Machine stitch down each side hem. Remove the basting and press the hems again. Turn up the bottom edge of the curtain 1½ in (4 cm) to the wrong side. Pin in place and press the fold.

4 Turn in a further 1½ in (4 cm) at the bottom edge of the curtain. Pin, baste, and remove the pins. Press the hem.

5 Machine stitch the bottom hem. Remove basting and press the bottom hem again.

6 Turn down the top edge 1½ in (4 cm) to the wrong side. Pin, baste, and remove the pins. Press the hem. Attach the heading tape, and gather and hang the curtain.

CAFÉ CURTAINS

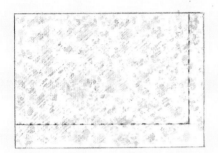

1 Cut a piece of fabric the width of the window plus 4 in (10 cm), by the drop length required plus 6 in (15 cm). Cut a strip 5 in (12.5 cm) wide and long enough to make enough loops. As a guide, one loop is placed at each end and then they are spaced approximately 4–6 in (10–15 cm) apart.

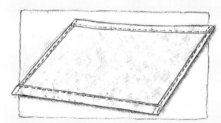

2 On the curtain piece make a hem, turning $\frac{5}{8}$ in (1.5 cm) twice down the sides and hem the top and bottom, turning 2 in (5 cm) twice. Fold the loop strip in half lengthwise with right sides together and machine stitch $\frac{1}{2}$ in (1.3 cm) from the raw edges. Press the seam open, placing it in the center of the strip.

3 Cut the loop strip into the desired lengths. Mark and stitch a point at one end of each piece. Trim excess fabric and turn right side out and press.

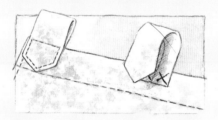

4 Place one loop at the end on the right side at the top of the curtain about 1 in (2.5 cm) down, bring the pointed end over to cover the raw edges. Baste and topstitch through all thicknesses. Position another loop at the other end of the curtain and space the remainder along evenly.

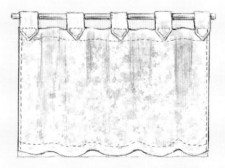

5 Thread the pole through the loops ready to hang at the window.

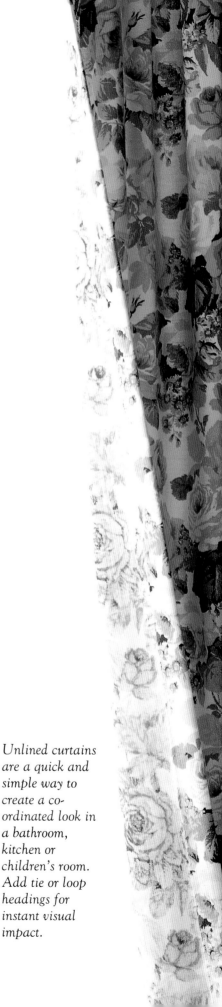

Unlined curtains are a quick and simple way to create a co-ordinated look in a bathroom, kitchen or children's room. Add tie or loop headings for instant visual impact.

TUBE-LINED CURTAINS

A lining protects the curtain fabric from the effects of sunlight and the dirt and dust from an open window. As tube-lining is done by machine it is a quick and easy method of lining curtains, and is ideal for a situation where the curtains may be changed frequently.

1 Stitch a line of basting to mark the hem allowances 3 in (7.5 cm) from the top and 4 in (10 cm) from the bottom of the curtain fabric.

2 Lay the fabric right side down and turn in each side edge 1⅜ in (3.5 cm) to the wrong side. Pin near the cut edges and press the folds. Remove the pins.

3 Lay the curtain fabric right side up and open out the pressed sides. Make a lengthwise fold in the fabric to take up the fullness, as the curtain is wider than the lining.

4 Place the lining right side down over the curtain, aligning the side edges and positioning the top and bottom of the lining 3 in (7.5 cm) from the cut edges of the curtain.

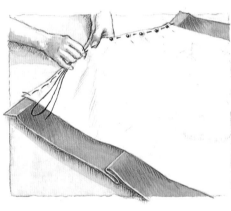

5 Pin the lining to the curtain at the sides. Baste together and remove the pins.

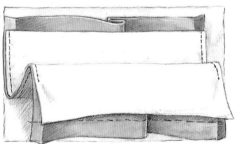

6 Machine stitch the side seams ⅜ in (1 cm) from the raw edges, starting at the top and ending 8 in (20 cm) from the bottom edge.

7 Turn right side out and press the side edges again. Baste the lining to the top of the curtain along the marked hemline.

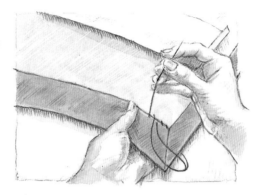

10 Form mitered corners at the bottom. Slipstitch the corners and the hem, and press.

8 Fold the top hem allowance over the top of the lining, pin, and press the fold in place. Remove the pins. Attach the heading tape.

11 Turn up 1 in (2.5 cm) twice for a double hem at the bottom of the lining and pin in place. Baste, remove the pins, machine stitch the hem, and press.

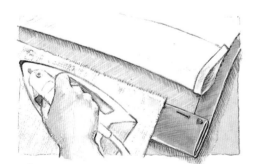

9 Turn up the bottom of the curtain fabric by 2 in (5 cm) twice to make a double hem. Pin in place and press. Remove the pins.

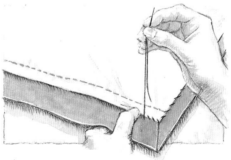

12 Slipstitch the loose lining to the sides of the curtain, and slipstitch along the hem for 1 in (2.5 cm) from each side. Gather the heading tape and hang the curtain.

A lined curtain but quickly made by machine, it is an ideal method for less expensive curtain fabrics. Add a lined valance to give a special touch.

LOCKED-IN LINING

Locked-in lining is done by hand and therefore takes a little bit longer, but it gives a better result, ensuring that the lining stays in place and hangs well with the curtain. This method is ideal for curtains that are expected to last a long time.

1 Lay the curtain fabric right side down and turn in each side edge 1½ in (4 cm) to the wrong side. Pin the sides near the cut edges and press the folds. Remove the pins.

2 Turn up 3 in (7.5 cm) twice across the bottom to form a double hem and pin in place. Press the hem and remove the pins.

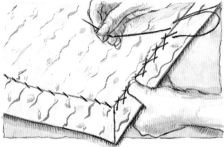

3 Form mitered corners at the bottom. Slipstitch the corners and the hem. Sew the side hems using a medium to large herringbone stitch. Press the sides, and hem.

4 Mark the hem allowance at the top of the curtain with a line of basting ⅝ in (1.5 cm) below the raw edge.

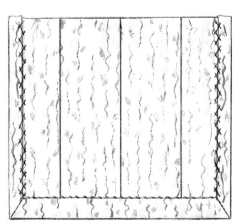

5 Mark vertical lines with tailor's chalk on the wrong side of the prepared curtain, drawing the first down the center, then marking further lines toward each side, spacing them about 12 in (30 cm) apart.

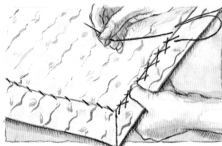

6 Turn up the bottom of the lining 2 in (5 cm) twice to form a double hem and pin in place. Machine stitch the hem and then press.

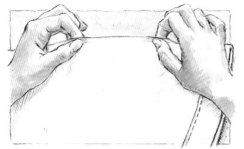

7 With right sides facing, fold the lining in half. Form a crease down the center from top to bottom.

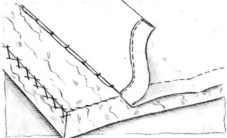

10 Lockstitch all the marked lines in the same way, working out from the center line and alternating from side to side.

8 Lay the curtain fabric right side down and place the lining wrong side down over it. Position the lining hem 1½ in (4 cm) above the curtain hem and align the raw edges of the lining with the side and top edges, matching the crease line and the center tailor's chalk line.

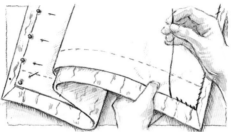

11 Smooth the lining toward the sides. Turn under the raw edges ¾ in (2 cm) and pin to the curtain side hems. Slipstitch the sides and along the hem for 1½ in (4 cm) from each side. Press the sides and hem.

9 Remove the pins. Fold back the lining. Work a loose lockstitch, starting 6 in (15 cm) from the top and ending 4 in (10 cm) from the bottom of the lining hem.

12 Pin and baste the lining and curtain fabric together across the top. Turn down the marked allowance and baste it in place. Attach the heading tape, gather and hang the curtain.

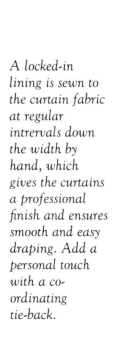

A locked-in lining is sewn to the curtain fabric at regular intrervals down the width by hand, which gives the curtains a professional finish and ensures smooth and easy draping. Add a personal touch with a co-ordinating tie-back.

LOCKED-IN INTERLINING

Curtains can be interlined by inserting a piece of thin wadding between curtain fabric and lining to provide extra insulation, reduce the amount of light filtering through, and help muffle outside noise. This method should be used with more expensive curtain fabrics as it gives a highly professional finish and helps to protect the curtain fabric from wear and tear.

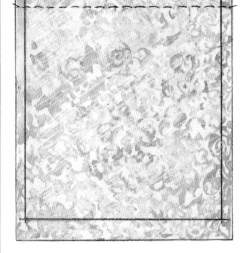

1 Lay the curtain fabric right side down. Mark the hem allowances: 3 in (7.5 cm) from the top with a line of basting, 2 in (5 cm) from the sides and 4 in (10 cm) from the bottom with tailor's chalk.

2 Mark a vertical line down the center of the curtain fabric using tailor's chalk. Working out from the center, mark lines 12 in (30 cm) apart out to the sides.

3 Place the interlining over the wrong side of the curtain fabric, with the cut edges against the marked hem allowances.

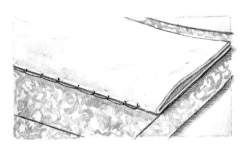

4 Fold back the interlining away from the center line and pin the interlining and fabric together. Work a loose lockstitch down the line, starting and finishing 3 in (7.5 cm) from the edge of the interlining.

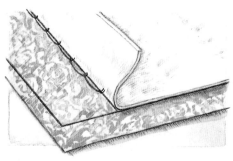

5 Lockstitch all vertical marked lines in the same way, working out from the center line and alternating from side to side, smoothing the interlining between each row before pinning.

6 Fold the hem allowances of the curtain sides and bottom hem over the interlining, pin and press. Form a miter at each bottom corner and slipstitch the mitered corners.

9 Fold the lining and pin it to the interlining 1 in (2.51 cm) from the center line of stitching, starting and finishing 6 in (15 cm) from the top and bottom. Lockstitch the lining to the interlining 1 in (2.5 cm) away from the previously lockstitched lines. Remove the pins.

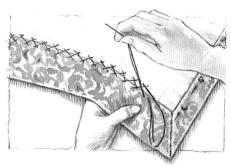

7 Herringbone stitch the sides and hem of the curtain to the interlining. Baste the curtain fabric and interlining together at the top.

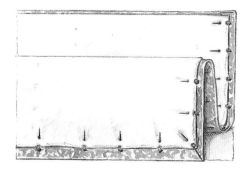

10 Smooth the lining toward the sides, top, and hem. Turn under the sides of the lining 1 in (2.5 cm) and the bottom 2 in (5 cm). Pin and then slipstitch to the sides and hem of the curtain. Remove the pins.

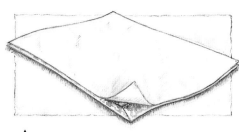

8 Place the lining wrong side down over the interlining, and align the raw edges with the edges of the interlined curtain.

11 Baste the lining and the curtain fabric together across the top. Turn down the marked allowance and pin in place. Press the fold and remove the pins. Attach the heading tape, gather and hang.

An interlined curtain is ideal for lounge or dining room curtains where a more luxurious fabric is being used. For a really glamorous look add matching or contrasting swags and tails.

DETACHABLE LINING

There are several advantages to detachable linings: they can be laundered separately, which is useful if they need frequent washing, they can be easily replaced, and they can be used to line an existing unlined curtain. The linings do not necessarily have to be as wide as the curtain itself. They are made in the same way as unlined curtains, but with a different type of heading tape.

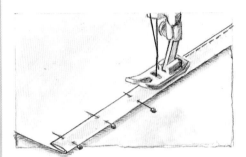

1 Lay the lining fabric right side down. Turn in each side edge $\frac{5}{8}$ in (1.5 cm) twice to the wrong side and pin in place. Machine stitch the sides close to the inside fold, removing the pins as you stitch. Press the sides.

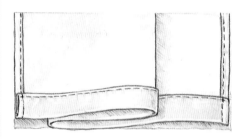

2 Turn up $1\frac{1}{2}$ in (4 cm) twice to the wrong side at the bottom and pin in place. Machine stitch across the bottom close to the upper fold, removing the pins as you stitch. Press the hem.

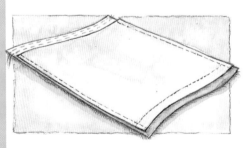

3 Check that the lining will be 1 in (2.5 cm) shorter than the curtain, keeping in mind that no seam allowance is needed at the top.

4 Slot the raw edge of the lining between the two flaps of the detachable lining heading tape, allowing an extra 1 in (2.5 cm) of tape at each side.

5 Knot the cords together at the sides that will meet at the center of the window.

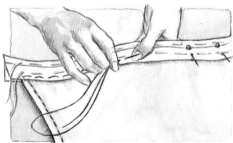

6 Pin and baste the tape in place, removing the pins as you work. Make sure that the lining fabric is completely enclosed by the tape.

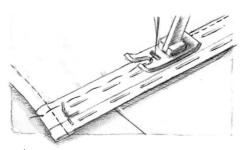

7 Fold each end of the tape over the side edge of the lining and stitch across the ends and along the lower edge of the tape. Remove the basting and press the lining.

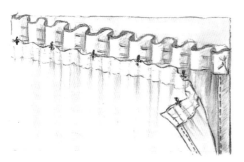

8 Pull up the free cords, gathering the lining until it is 2 in (5 cm) narrower than the curtain. Insert the hooks into the lining heading tape, then into the curtain tape, to attach the two layers together.

9 Attach the lining to the curtain at intervals down the sides, either with catchstitches, or by hand-sewing strips of touch-and-close fastener to the curtain and lining.

A detachable lining is quick and easy to make for an existing unlined curtain, a temporary curtain, or for a curtain fabric that is dry clean only. Add a special touch with a quick swag in matching fabric.

SHEER CURTAINS

'Sheer' is a description given to very lightweight fabrics, they are translucent to varying degrees and range from muslin to lace. Generally, a fullness from two to three times the width of the window is required. You can buy sheer fabric to make your own curtains, see Method One, or you can adapt ready-to-hang curtains, see Method Two. Methods Three and Four use fabric with finished side edges some of which has an extra detachable border edge used to trim the bottom hem.

C H E C K   L I S T

Materials

Techniques

Method One

1 Cut the fabric into drop lengths and trim off the selvage. Join lengths with French seams if necessary to get the required width.

2 Turn in ⅜ in (1 cm) twice to the wrong side to make a double hem down each side and pin in place. Machine stitch the hems and remove the pins as you stitch.

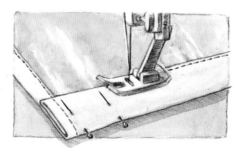

3 Turn up 1 in (2.5 cm) twice to the wrong side to form a double hem at the bottom and pin in place. Machine stitch the hem and remove the pins as you stitch.

4 Make the casing at the top by turning under ⅜ in (1 cm) and pin in place. Press the fold and remove the pins.

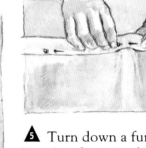

5 Turn down a further 1½ in (4 cm) and pin in place. Press the fold and machine stitch close to the bottom edge of the hem, removing the pins as you stitch.

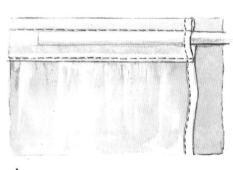

6 Work another row of stitching ⅜ in (1 cm) from the top edge. Thread the wire or rod through the channel between the two rows of stitching.

Method Two

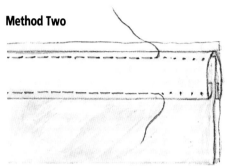

1 Before making the side hems, you need to unpick the applied heading for 1 in (2.5 cm) on each side. Follow Step 2, Method One, to make double hems down each side.

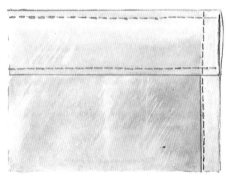

2 Trim off $\frac{3}{8}$ in (1 cm) from each side of the heading, turn under $\frac{3}{8}$ in (1 cm) to finish, and machine back in place.

Method Three

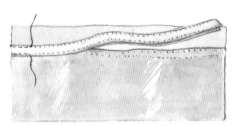

To shorten this type of curtain fabric, unpick and take off the heading. Trim off from the top edge to give the correct drop measurement. Make the side hems and re-stitch the heading, finishing the ends as in steps above.

Method Four

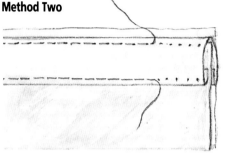

1 Make the casing across the top following steps 4, 5, and 6 Method One.

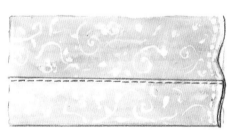

2 Make a double bottom hem as shown in step 3, Method One, *or* if your lace fabric has a removable extra side border, continue with steps 3 and 4.

3 Remove the border by pulling it off. Turn up $\frac{1}{4}$ in (6 mm) to the right side at the bottom of the curtain. Baste the hem in place and then press it.

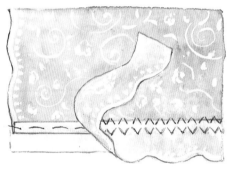

4 Machine stitch the border lace over the hem using zigzag stitch and matching thread. Finish the edges in line with the sides.

TIP BOX

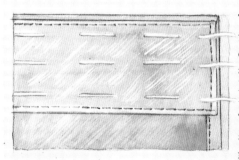

To use heading tape and hooks for a track with runners or the direct contact-fixing method, add only $2\frac{3}{8}$ in (6 cm) to the length, for the hem, and follow instructions 1–3.

Turn $\frac{3}{8}$ in (1 cm) to the wrong side and place the heading tape $\frac{1}{8}$ in (3 mm) from the top edge. Stitch in place according to the manufacturer's instructions.

CURTAIN ACCESSORIES

Curtain accessories such as tiebacks and valances add a special finishing touch and help to create a fully coordinated look. This section gives a choice of tiebacks – ruched, plaited, and edged – one of which will suit most room settings. Tiebacks can be made to match the curtains, or they can link with other items in the room. A formal or gathered valance, with contact heading tape for a quick and easy fixing method, is also explained here, as well as instructions for making a single swag and pleated tails.

QUICKIE TIEBACKS

Tiebacks are an ideal way to coordinate your curtains with other furnishings in the room. This tieback is quick and easy to make with a heading tape across a double piece of fabric.

1 For each tieback, cut out a piece of fabric 10 in (25 cm) wide by twice the required finished length.

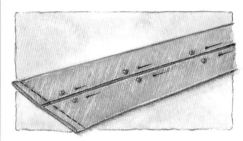

2 Turn in each long side of the strip of fabric to the right side so that the raw edges meet down the center, and pin in place. Machine in stitch across each end. Remove the pins, turn right side out and press.

4 Pull up the cords of the tape until the tieback is the required length. Tie the cords securely and tuck them away at the back.

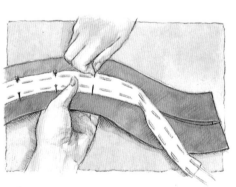

3 Pin the heading tape in place over the raw edges, turning under ½ in (1.2 cm) at each end of the tape to finish. Machine stitch, working in the same direction along both edges. Remove the pins as you stitch.

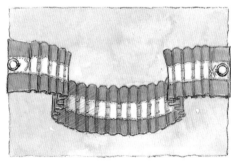

5 Blanket-stitch the curtain rings to the reverse side of the tieback, about ¾ in (2 cm) from each end.

EDGED TIEBACK

This style of tieback goes well with a valance and consists of a crescent-shaped piece of fusible buckram covered with fabric. A decorative binding is added all round the edge and the material used for the binding could match the valance material or coordinate with other furnishings in the room. You can buy a ready-made shape or use the template given on page 154.

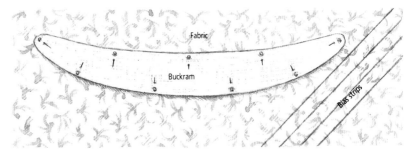

1 Cut out the main fabric using the crescent-shaped piece of buckram as a guide. Cut bias strips 1 in (2.5 cm) wide for the binding. Join the strips to make sufficient length to go all around the shape.

2 Position the buckram on the wrong side of a piece of lining, and place the cut tieback right side up over the buckram. Press with a hot iron and damp press cloth to fuse them together. Trim off the surplus lining fabric around the buckram shape, taking care not to cut into the buckram.

3 Fold $\frac{1}{4}$ in (6 mm) to the wrong side at one end of the strip of binding. With right sides facing and raw edges even, pin the turned-in edge of the binding to the curve of the tieback and continue pinning all around.

4 Machine stitch binding to tieback $\frac{1}{4}$ in (6 mm) from the edge all the way around, turning under and overlapping remaining raw edge of binding. Remove pins as you stitch.

5 Fold binding over the raw edge of the tieback to the back. Turn the raw edge of the binding under by $\frac{1}{4}$ in (6 mm) and slipstitch to the lining. Blanket stitch the rings to the reverse side of the tieback, about $\frac{3}{4}$ in (2 cm) from each end.

PLAITED TIE-BACK

Three padded fabric tubes are plaited together to make this attractive tie-back. It looks best if two of the tubes are made in the same fabric and the third in a contrasting color. Or, make two strips in a plain fabric and the third in a patterned fabric echoing another material in the room.

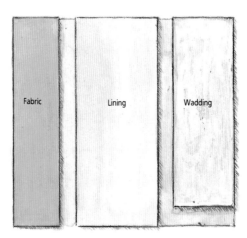

1 For each tieback, cut three fabric strips 4 in (10 cm) wide by 1½ times the required finished length. Cut three lining strips 6 in (15 cm) wide by the same length as the fabric. Cut three pieces of batting 4¾ in (12 cm) wide and 1½ in (4 cm) shorter than the lining.

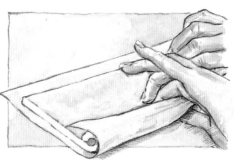

2 Place the batting against the wrong side of the lining, with the edges aligned on one long edge. Roll up the lining and batting together.

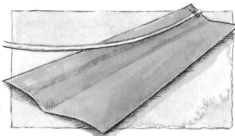

4 Secure a length of piping cord to the main fabric strip by machine stitching it to one short end, on the right side.

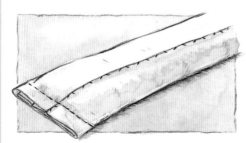

3 Turn under ⅜ in (1 cm) on the remaining long edge of the lining and slipstitch down along the center of the roll. Stitch across the ends with a small basting stitch.

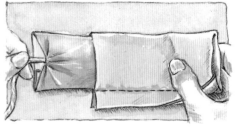

5 Fold the strip in half lengthwise, right sides together, enclosing the cord. Machine stitch the raw edges together along the long side. Turn right side out by pulling the cord, then cut the cord close to the fabric edge.

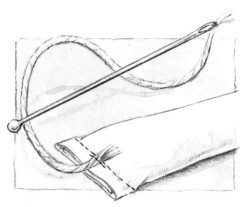

6 Stitch one end of the cord to the padded roll and the other to a large-eyed, long blunt needle or bodkin.

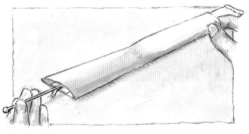

7 Insert the needle/bodkin into the fabric tube at one end and pull the padded roll through it. Cut off the cord. Repeat steps 2–7 to make the other two padded strips.

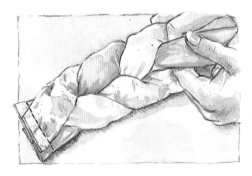

8 Stitch the three padded strips together, overlapping them at one end, and then plait them. Stitch them together at the other end to hold the plait securely. Check the tieback for size.

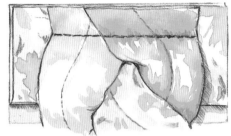

9 Bind each end with a 4 in (10 cm) square piece of main fabric. Fold the square in half, wrong sides together. Align the raw edges with those at the end of the plait and machine stitch together.

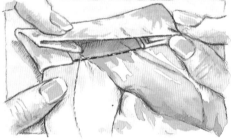

10 Fold in one end of the binding square, then the other. Turn the folded edge over to cover the machine stitching and slipstitch securely. Remember to make the folds on the same side at each end of the plait.

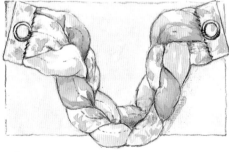

11 Blanket-stitch the rings to the reverse side of the tieback, about ¾ in (2 cm) from each end.

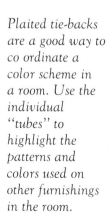

Plaited tie-backs are a good way to co ordinate a color scheme in a room. Use the individual "tubes" to highlight the patterns and colors used on other furnishings in the room.

RUFFLED TIEBACK

This style of tieback is made with pre-cut iron-on interfacing and could be co-ordinated with a valance or frilled cushions by using a matching or contrasting material for the ruffle. Iron-on interfacing is used to stiffen the tieback to give it a professional look. Cut the frilly strip in one piece if possible. If it is not possible to do this, cut shorter strips and join them with open seams to get the required length.

CHECKLIST

Materials

crescent-shaped iron-on interfacing
fabric
fabric strip
lining
two rings
general sewing equipment · · · · · · · · page 134

Techniques

pressing	page 137
open seams	page 142
machine stitching	page 140
slipstitch	page 139
blanket stitch	page 139

Measuring up

See page 154.

1 Using the interfacing shape as a guide, cut out the main fabric for each tieback, adding $\frac{5}{8}$ in (1.5 cm) turning allowance all around. For the ruffle, cut a strip 6 in (15 cm) wide by twice the measurement along the bottom of the interfacing.

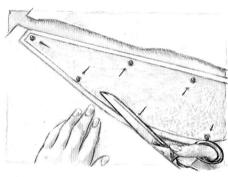

2 Cut out the lining using the interfacing as a pattern again and adding $\frac{1}{4}$ in (6 mm) seam allowance all around.

3 Position the interfacing with the adhesive side facing the wrong side of the main fabric, making sure that the seam allowance is even all around. Press in position.

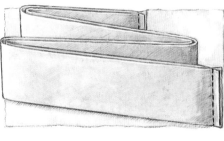

4 Join strips of fabric if necessary to make the required length of ruffle. With right sides facing, fold the ruffle strip in half lengthwise, and machine stitch across each end. Turn right side out and press.

5 Work two rows of machine gathering, $\frac{5}{8}$ in (1.5 cm) and $\frac{1}{4}$ in (6 mm) from the raw edge of the ruffle. Mark the center and pull up the threads, gathering the ruffle to fit the bottom of the tieback $\frac{5}{8}$ in (1.5 cm) in from each end.

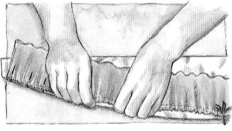

6 Mark the center of the tieback. Place the ruffle over the front of the tieback, matching the center marks and with the ruffle $\frac{5}{8}$ in (1.5 cm) from each end. Align the raw edges with the bottom edge of the tieback and pin in place.

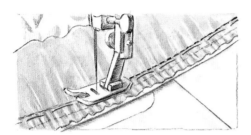

7 Even out the gathers and baste the ruffle to the tieback, keeping the stitches close to the edge of the interfacing. Remove pins and stitch the ruffle in place.

Tiebacks are ideal for bedrooms or pretty cottage-style rooms. If in a bedroom, coordinate with frilled pillowcases. For a plain curtain fabric, make the tieback in a patterned material for a splash of color.

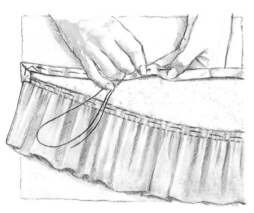

8 Trim the seam. Turn the ruffle down and baste. Turn and baste the seam allowance along the straight edge and sides.

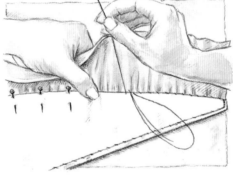

10 Place the lining wrong side down on the reverse side of the tieback. Pin and then slipstitch the lining in place.

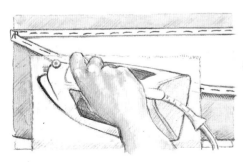

9 Prepare the lining by turning under to the wrong side $\frac{3}{8}$ in (1 cm) all around. Baste in place and then press.

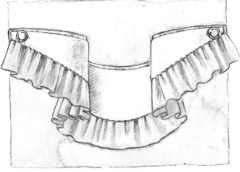

11 Blanket stitch the rings to the reverse side of the tieback about $\frac{3}{4}$ in (2 cm) from each end.

RUCHED TIEBACK

A padded fabric roll is made in the same way as for the plaited tieback, and this is inserted into a longer tube of fabric, which is then gathered up to create an elegant ruched effect.

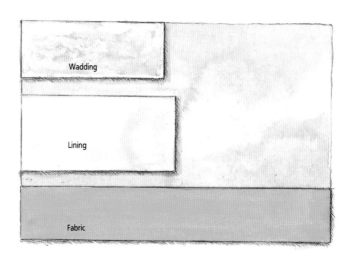

1 For each tieback, cut out a strip of the main fabric 6 in (15 cm) wide by twice the required finished length. Cut out the lining 8 in (20 cm) wide by the final length required. Cut out the batting 6½ in (16 cm) wide and 1¼ in (3 cm) shorter than the lining.

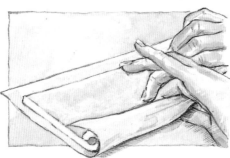

2 Place the batting against the wrong side of the lining, with the edges aligned on one long edge. Roll up the lining and batting together.

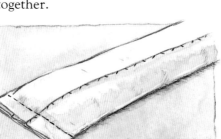

3 Turn under ⅜ in (1 cm) on the remaining long edge of the lining and slipstitch down along the center of the roll. Stitch across the ends with a small basting stitch.

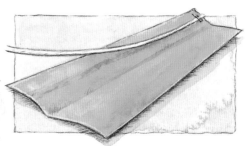

4 Secure a length of piping cord to the main fabric strip by machine stitching it to one short end, on the right side.

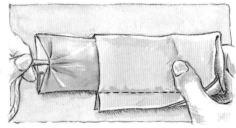

5 Fold the strip in half lengthwise, right sides together, enclosing the cord. Machine stitch the raw edges together along the long side. Turn right side out by pulling the cord, then cut the cord close to the fabric edge.

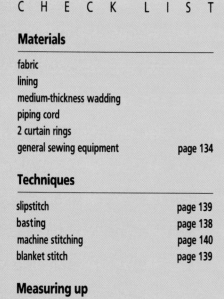

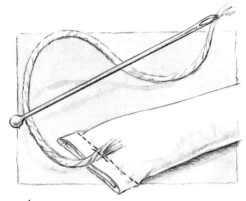

6 Stitch one end of the cord to the padded roll and the other to a large-eyed, long blunt needle or bodkin.

For that special touch, a ruched tieback in a single fabric adds texture and visual impact. Use a contrasting fabric or, for a plain curtain, make the tieback in the same material as the main upholstery.

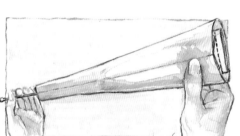

7 Insert the needle/bodkin into the fabric tube at one end. Pull the padded roll through the tube until the end of the roll is level with the beginning of the fabric tube.

9 Keep pulling the cord, ruching the fabric at the same time, until the padded roll emerges at the other end. Pin in place, then cut off the cord close to the edge and finish the end as in step 8.

8 Finish the end of the tube by turning in the two corners. Then turn the end over twice and slipstitch neatly. Make sure the roll is securely attached to the end of the fabric tube.

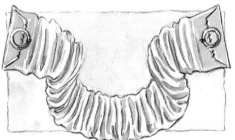

10 Blanket-stitch the rings to the reverse side of the tieback about ¾ in (2 cm) from each end.

SINGLE SWAG

The instructions given here
are for a single swag. Make a
sample swag and tail using
lining fabric or sheeting
to help calculate the fabric.

C H E C K L I S T

Materials

fabric see below
lining see below
touch-and-close fastener
general sewing equipment   page 134

Techniques

cutting	page 136
basting	page 138
slipstitch	page 138
zigzag stitch	page 141
pressing	page 137
attaching touch-and-close fastener	page 146

Measuring

Measure the length of the valance board, the
returns from wall to wall, and the curtain drop.
The finished top of the swag should equal the
length of the board, and the drop should be
approximately one-sixth of the curtain drop. Once
you have decided on the finished size of the swag,
follow the diagram for the proportions

A to B = ½ finished width

C to D = 2½ times finished drop

E to F = 1½ times finished width. Note that this line
is three-quarters of the way down from the top of
the cut drop measurement.

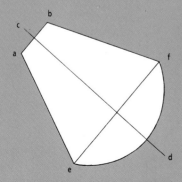

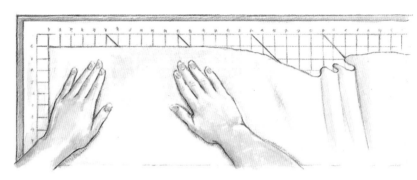

1 Place the lining right side down
on a cutting board or squared
paper, and align the selvage with a
straight line along the length of the
board.

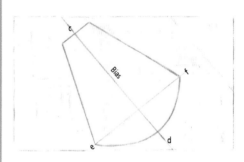

2 Mark the swag shape on the
lining with tailor's chalk or fabric
pen, starting with the bias line CD
and following the dimensions on
the Measuring diagram. Add a seam
allowance of ½ in (1.2 cm) on the
curved edge.

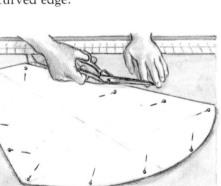

3 Cut out the shape and use it to
cut the main fabric, making sure
that the center line is on the bias.
Cut a binding strip 4 in (10 cm)
deep by the width of the finished
swag plus 1¼ in (3 cm).

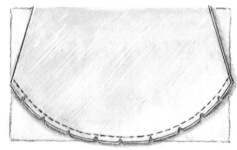

4 With right sides together,
machine stitch the lining and fabric
along the curve, ½ in (1.2 cm) from
the raw edges. Trim the seam and
notch it, turn right side out, and
press. Baste the sides and top.

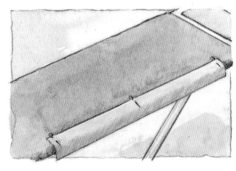

5 Pin the binding strip to a
suitable surface such as an ironing
board, with the long side projecting
1 in (2.5 cm) over the edge. Mark
the center point and a seam
allowance of ⅝ in (1.5 cm) at each
end with pins.

6 Mark the center point of the swag and pin the swag to the strip, matching the centers. Pleat the long sides evenly up to the binding strip starting at point F and working on one side at a time.

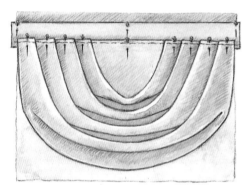

7 About four pleats on each side will take up the fullness of the material. The pleats on each side of center will be across the straight top edge of the swag and points E and F will touch the end pins.

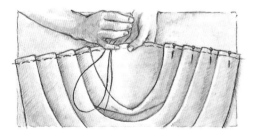

8 Unpin the swag from the binding strip, but replace the pins to hold the pleats as you work across. Baste the pleats in place.

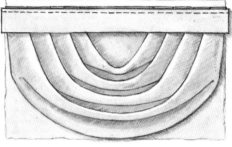

9 With right sides together, place the binding strip along the top of the swag and pin in place. Baste and remove the pins. Machine stitch $\frac{1}{2}$ in (1.2 cm) from the raw edges.

10 Fold the seam and binding strip to the wrong side. Turn in $\frac{5}{8}$ in (1.5 cm) at the sides and $\frac{1}{2}$ in (1.2 cm) along the length. Fold the binding down and slipstitch to cover the stitching.

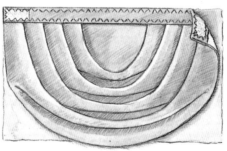

11 Zigzag stitch the loop side of the touch-and-close fastener tape to the wrong side of the binding. Stitch a 6 in (15 cm) length of the hook side of touch-and-close fastener to the right side at each side of the swag to hold the tails.

QUICK SWAG

For a quick and easy, yet no less stunning, effect, make a simple unlined swag. Measure the length of the pole and the drop on each side and make extra allowance for the required depth of the drape. The simplest way to calculate the amount of fabric needed is to take a length of string and loop it over the pole to imitate the swag.

1 Cut out the fabric and trim away the selvages. Drape the length of fabric over the pole to assess the effect when the full width is used. Reduce the depth if necessary by cutting the excess from one long edge of the fabric.

2 Make a double hem all around the outside edges by turning $\frac{1}{4}$ in (6 mm) to the wrong side twice, then pin it in place. Baste the hem, remove the pins, machine stitch close to the basting, and press.

TAILS

Instructions are given for a left-hand tail. To make the right-hand one, reverse the pattern when you cut out the fabric. The tails overlap the swag at each end by 6 in (15 cm).

CHECK LIST

Materials

fabric see below
lining in contrasting color see below
touch-and-close fastener
self-adhesive "hook" tape
general sewing equipment   page 134

Techniques

cutting   page 136
slipstitch   page 139
machine stitching   page 140
pressing   page 137
attaching touch-and-close fastener   page 146

Measuring

Note the measurements required following the diagram.
A to B = the drop of the finished swag.
C to D = A to B times 2
C to D and D to F = width of a return (generally 4 in/10 cm).
The instructions are for three pleats using 8 in (20 cm) of fabric per pleat. The fold of the first pleat is placed on the inside edge of the return and the second and third 1 in (2.5 cm) away from the previous pleat.

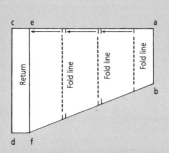

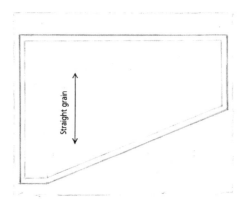

1 Lay the lining fabric right side down and mark the dimensions of the tail piece with tailor's chalk or fabric pen, adding a seam allowance of $\frac{1}{2}$ in (1.2 cm) all around.

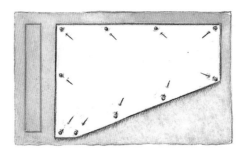

2 Cut out the shape and use this to cut the main fabric. Cut a binding strip 4 in (10 cm) deep by the width of the finished tail.

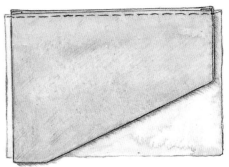

4 Turn right side out and press the edges. Baste the fabric and lining together across the raw top edge.

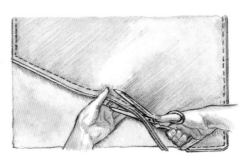

3 Place the main fabric and lining right sides together, and machine stitch around the sides and bottom edge $\frac{1}{2}$ in (1.2 cm) from the raw edges. Trim the seams and corners.

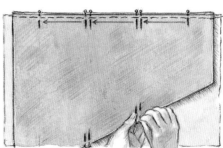

5 Mark the position of the pleats and the spaces between them with pins along the top and bottom edges of the tail following the measurements given.

6 Form three pleats, starting at the short edge, pressing them in place as you go. Press a fold down the line (E to F) where the tail will turn around the corner of the valance board.

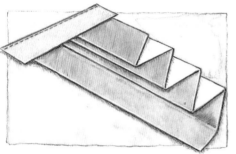

7 Place the binding strip right side down across the right side of the top of the tail and pin in place. Baste, removing the pins as you work. Machine stitch $\frac{1}{2}$ in (1.2 cm) from the raw edges.

8 Press the seam and strip upward on the wrong side. Turn in $\frac{5}{8}$ in (1.5 cm) at the sides and $\frac{1}{2}$ in (1.2 cm) along the length. Fold the binding down and slipstitch in place, covering the machine stitching.

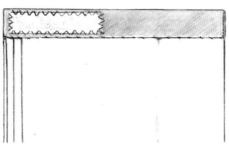

9 Machine stitch the loop side of the touch-and-close fastener tape to the wrong side of the binding across the front face of the tail using zigzag stitch.

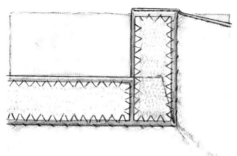

10 Make a diagonal fold in the binding to form a corner for the side return and attach a strip of fastener with zigzag stitch to the wrong side of the side return.

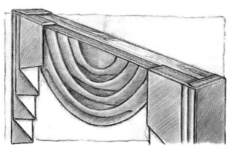

11 Make a right-hand side tail in the same way, but reversing the sides on the diagram.

HANGING A SWAG AND TAILS

Press the hook side of the touch-and-close fastener to the top of the valance board and the returns. Place the swag in position and press the fastener tape on the swag firmly against the tape on the board. Then attach the tails over the swag to the top of the board at each side and around the returns. A thumbtack at each side will keep them securely in position.

VALANCES

The instructions given here on how to make a valance uses a double-sided self-adhesive stiffener, which is an easy method that produces good results. A variety of shapes are printed on the peel-off backing paper.

Measuring up

To estimate how big your pelmet is, measure the length of the pelmet board from A to B and the returns, B to C, plus the depth, D to E.

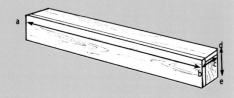

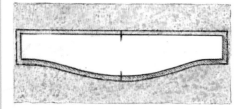

1 Cut out the fabric using the stiffener as a template, adding ¾ in (2 cm) all around. Mark the center points of both fabric and stiffener. stiffener.

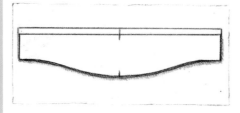

2 Cut out the lining to the exact size of the stiffener shape at the bottom and sides, but add an extra 1 in (2.5 cm) at the top.

3 Start peeling the backing paper from the stiffener, working from the center. Place the fabric wrong side down on the adhesive, matching centers. Continue to peel away the backing, smoothing down the fabric with your hand as you go to prevent puckering.

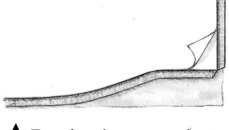

4 Turn the valance over and snip the curves of the hem allowance, but not right up to the edge of the stiffener. Cut the corners away. Peel the backing paper from the reverse side of the stiffener.

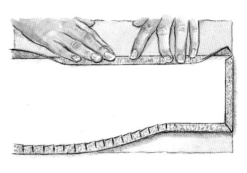

5 Press down the turning allowance with your fingers, making neat miters at the corners.

6 Turn 1 in (2.5 cm) at the top and ⅜ in (9 mm) along the bottom and the sides to the wrong side of the lining and press in place.

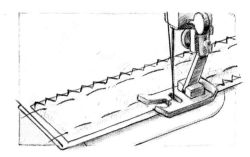

7 Position a strip of the loop side of the self-adhesive fastener along the right-side top edge of the lining. Machine stitch with zigzag stitch along both edges of the fastener.

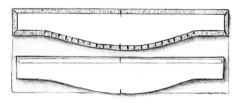

8 Mark the center of the lining on the right side, and the valance on the wrong side.

9 Place the lining carefully over the back of the valance, wrong side down, aligning the center marks. Smooth the lining on the adhesive as before. Slipstitch the lining to the fabric around the edges.

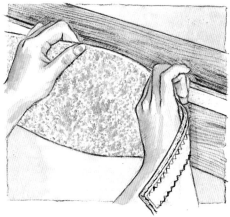

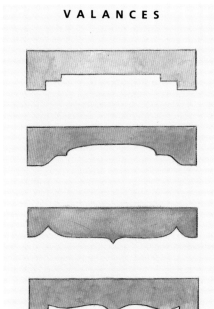

10 Press the hook side of the self-adhesive fastener to the front edge of the valance board. Starting in the center, attach the valance by firmly pressing together the self-adhesive fastener.

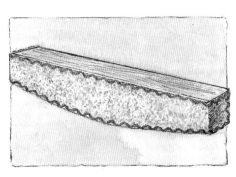

11 If desired, add coordinating trimming braid using fabric glue once the valance is in position.

VALANCES

Valances give an added dimension to windows whatever the size and style of the room. Choose a shape that suits the room, from a simple square to the more elaborate styles used for larger windows and more exotic, heavier draperies. Above is a selection of possible valance shapes. You may want the shape of the valance to echo a shape in the curtain fabric. However, whatever size or style you choose, always make sure there is enough space between the valance and the curtain track to allow the curtains to be opened and closed freely.

Once you have chosen your valance, cover it in a fabric that either matches or contrasts with the curtains and coordinates with other fabrics in the room.

VALANCES

Valances are like mini curtains. To determine the desired length, cut a length of paper or spare fabric about one-sixth of the curtain drop and tape it to the curtain to check the effect.

CHECKLIST

Materials

fabric	page 54
lining	
pencil pleat heading tape with loop backing	
self-adhesive hook tape	
general sewing equipment	page 134

Techniques

cutting	page 136
open seams	page 142
mitered corners	page 144
machine stitching	page 140
pressing	page 137
slipstitch	page 139
basting	page 138
attaching heading tape	page 52

Measuring

Measure the length of the valance shelf or track, and the returns from wall to wall. Calculate the width of fabric needed to give the correct fullness in the same way as for curtains. Decide on the depth of the valance in proportion to the length of the curtains and add 1½ in (4 cm).

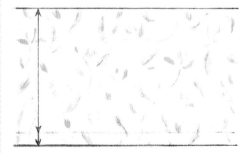

1 Cut out the required number of widths from the curtain fabric, adding 1½ in (4 cm) to the finished depth. Cut out lining to the size of the finished valance, omitting hem allowances. Join widths of fabric and lining if necessary.

2 Lay the fabric right side down and turn in 1 in (2.5 cm) along the bottom and side edges. Pin in place. Press and remove the pins. Form a miter in each bottom corner.

3 Machine stitch the miters from the fold to ⅜ in (1 cm) from the raw edges. Trim the corner away. Turn the valance right side out and press the corners again.

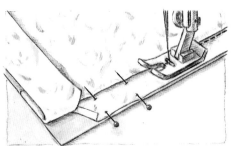

4 With the lining right side up, place the valance over it, right side down. Align the bottom raw edges, and pin them together. Machine stitch ⅜ in (1 cm) from the edges and remove pins.

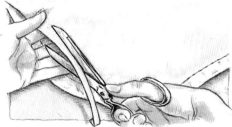

5 Turn the lining over to the wrong side of the valance and press the fold. Trim off ¼ in (6 mm) from the sides and top edge of the lining.

6 Turn the lining under by ⅜ in (1 cm) at the sides. Pin the side hems, slipstitch, then press.

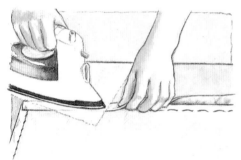

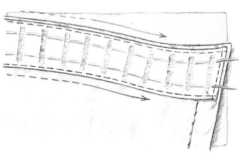

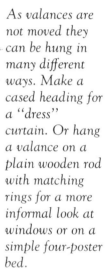

7 Baste down the lining, which should be ⅝ in (1.5 cm) shorter than the valance, along the top. Turn the ⅝ in (1.5 cm) heading allowance over the lining and press the fold.

9 Machine stitch along the tape, working in the same direction along both edges and stitch the turned-in ends. Gather the valance to the required length by pulling up the cords. Knot the ends and tuck them away at the back.

As valances are not moved they can be hung in many different ways. Make a cased heading for a "dress" curtain. Or hang a valance on a plain wooden rod with matching rings for a more informal look at windows or on a simple four-poster bed.

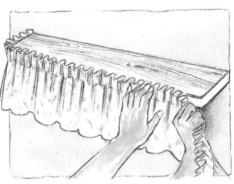

8 Position the heading tape just below the top of the valance, and turn ⅝ in (1.5 cm) under at each end of the tape. Make sure the cords are free. Pin the tape in place.

10 Attach the self-adhesive hook side of the tape to the front edge of the valance shelf and press the loop backing of the heading tape to it, starting in the center and working outward.

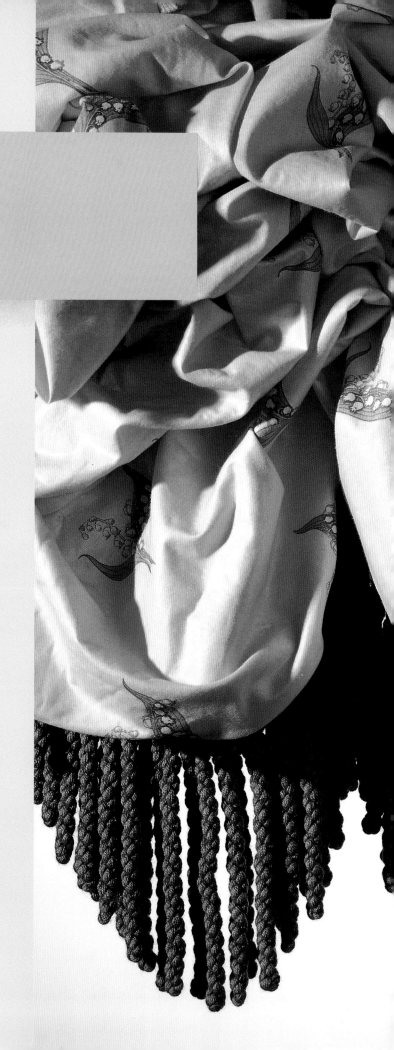

SHADES

Shades are a practical and economical way of covering windows. This section gives instructions for Roman, balloon, and festoon shades. The Roman shade has a flat tailored appearance, making it an ideal choice above a kitchen sink or a countertop, and when raised, it allows maximum daylight to enter the room. The balloon shade has inverted pleats which when raised balloon out quite magically. The extra fullness from the gathered heading of a festoon shade gives a more luxurious appearance.

MEASURING FOR SHADES

SHADES ARE often a more practical alternative to window dressing than curtains – they use less fabric and are relatively simple to make.

Absolute accuracy at all stages is essential when measuring, but especially when cutting the fabric, if the shade is to hang true. Lining is advisable, as it makes the finished shade hang better, protects the fabric, and improves insulation.

Note the instructions for measuring different types of shades to figure out positions for the seams that make them as unobtrusive as possible.

When working with joined fabrics, make sure that the seams of the lining correspond exactly with those of the main fabric to avoid an unsightly appearance when light shows through from the back.

For the Roman shade, if you do need to make seams in the fabric to obtain the correct width required, make sure you have a full width in the center, with the extra fabric joined on each side.

The three shades shown in this section hang in slightly different ways, though the finishing methods are similar. It is important to choose a fabric appropriate to the style of shade – firmly woven curtain fabric is ideal for Roman or balloon shades, while light/medium-weight material is better suited to ruche and form the swags that distinguish a festoon shade.

Positioning the batten

All the shades in this section are attached at the top of the window to a wooden batten. Each shade is pulled up by a series of vertical cords threaded through rings sewn on the reverse side. When the shade is raised, the cords are secured by winding them in a figure-eight around a cleat which is screwed to the side wall. To conceal the batten, paint it or cover in coordinating fabric.

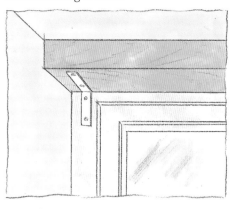

For the batten, you will need a 1 × 2 in (25 × 50 mm) piece of softwood, cut to the required length and attached to the wall at the top of the window with angle brackets.

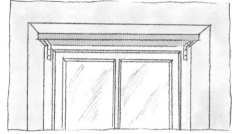

For fitting within a recess, the shade should be made 1 in (2.5 cm) narrower, so that it will fit neatly inside it. The batten should then be attached to the ceiling of the recess, (not suitable for a balloon shade) and the drop of the shade measured from the ceiling to the sill.

If the batten is to be set on the wall above the window, cut the batten long enough to extend 2 in (5 cm) on each side.

Measuring

To calculate the finished width of the shade, measure the length of the batten.

• To calculate the finished **length** of the shade, measure from the top of the batten to the sill. For a shade set inside a recess, deduct ¾ in (2 cm) to allow for clearance above the sill. If it is to be positioned outside the window, add 4 in (10 cm), so the shade will fall that distance from the bottom of the sill.

• Check your measurements at several points on the window frame to make sure it is square.

ROMAN SHADES

TO FORM THE DISTINCTIVE pleats of a Roman shade, horizontal channels are stitched at regular intervals down its length, through which narrow rods or laths are inserted. These give a more professional-looking, tailored appearance when the shade is pulled up.

• Calculate the finished length and width of the shade, and add 1 in (2.5 cm) allowances all around.

• For the lining, the width will be exactly the same as the finished width of the shade, but extra length is required to allow for the channels, which are stitched across the lining to hold the laths or rods. This extra length is based on how many channels you want.

• To calculate the exact number of channels needed for the size of your shade, make a plan (see left), dividing the length into sections as follows: mark the first line 6 in (15 cm) up from the bottom, mark the center lines 12 in (30 cm) apart, and allow an extra 3 in (8 cm) above the position of the final one for the top section. You may need to adjust the sizes of the spaces slightly to accommodate the finished length of the shade.

• Once you have decided on the number of channels, add an extra $2\frac{1}{4}$ in (6 cm) to the length for each one. (Note: the size of the channel quoted here allows for the use of $1 \times \frac{1}{8}$ in (25×4 mm) wooden laths. If you are using wooden or plastic rods with a diameter of less than 1 in (2.5 cm), reduce the size of the channels accordingly.) Finally, add a further 1 in (2.5 cm) top hem allowance to give you the total length for the lining fabric.

HANGING THE SHADE

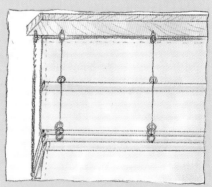

Attach screw eyes to the batten so that they correspond exactly with the rows of rings on the shade. Attach an extra one 1 in (2.5 cm) from the edge of the batten on the operating side.

• Attach the hook side of the fastener tape to the front and press the tapes together to position the shade. Thread the cords through the screw eyes and knot them together just outside the last one. Cut the ends level, and attach a cord pull to hold the cord ends together. Screw the cleat in position on the wall.

3 in (8 cm)

12 in (30 cm)

12 in (30 cm)

12 in (30 cm)

12 in (30 cm)

6 in (15 cm)

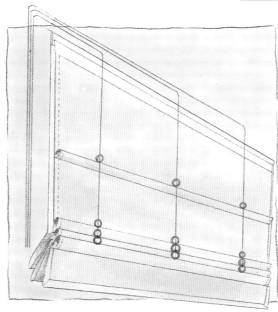

BALLOON SHADES

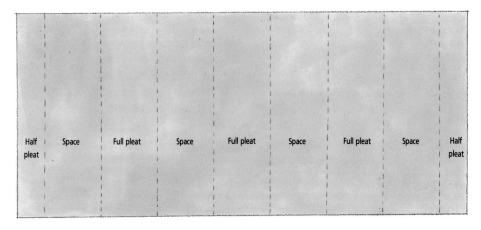

Half pleat · Space · Full pleat · Space · Full pleat · Space · Full pleat · Space · Half pleat

TO CREATE THE FULLNESS needed for the inverted pleats of a balloon shade, it will be necessary to join widths of fabric. By carefully planning the positioning of the pleats, the seam lines can be concealed by a fold. The allowance for the length takes into account the extra fabric required for the bottom swags which are ruched permanently.

• Follow the guidance for Positioning The Batten and note the finished width and length required for the shade.

• Make a plan (see right) for the position of the pleats, allowing 12 in (30 cm) for a full pleat and 6 in (15 cm) for the half pleats on each side of the shade. Allow a 12 in (30 cm) space between the center of each pleat and divide the finished width of the shade by this measurement to give you the number of pleats that will be required. You may need to adjust the measurements slightly to accommodate the finished width in relation to the width of fabric used – make your alteration to the size allowed for the spaces rather than the pleats.

• Once you have calculated the width of fabric required, add 3¼ in (8 cm) for side hems and 1¼ in (3 cm) for each joining seam. Add 12 in (30 cm) to the finished drop measurement.

• The measurement for the lining fabric is the same as the curtain fabric.

Roman shade

Balloon shade

FESTOON SHADES

FESTOON SHADES have a more lavish appearance, due to their extra fullness – at least twice the width of the batten is needed. If it is necessary to join widths, the seams will be less obtrusive if they are joined where a row of rings will be sewn. Note, the length allowance takes into account the extra fabric for the bottom swags.

• Follow the guidance for positioning the batten and note the finished width and length required for the shade.

• You will need at least twice the width in fabric and an extra 12 in (30 cm) (see right) added to the length. Allow a 24 in (60 cm) space between the rings in the ungathered material, and add a further 2 in (5 cm) on each side. Bear in mind the approximate position of the rings before working out the quantity of fabric and where the

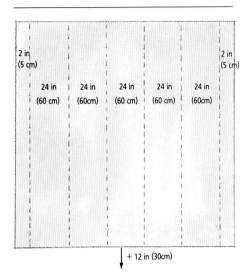

seams will be. If ruffles are to be added, remember to make allowance by reducing the length measurement of the shade by the depth of the ruffle, but allow enough fabric to make the ruffle.

• The measurement for the lining is the same as the main fabric.

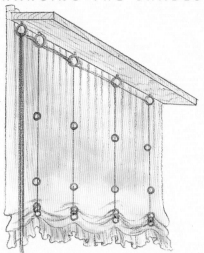

Attach screw eyes to the batten so that they correspond exactly with the rows of rings on the shade. Fix an extra screw 1 in (2.5 cm) from the edge on the operating side (left or right) of the shade. For a balloon shade, attach the hook side of the fastener to the top of the batten and press the tapes together to position the shade so that it hangs over the edge. For a festoon shade, attach the hook side of the fastener to the front of the batten and pull up the heading tape cords.

• Thread the cords through the screw eyes, and knot them together just outside the last one. Even off the ends, plait the loose cords if desired, and attach a cord pull to hold the cord ends together. Screw the cleat in position on the wall. To keep the bottom permanently ruched, raise the shade to the desired drop measurement and wind the cords around the cleat. Tie or sew two or more rings together on the vertical rows.

Festoon shade

ROMAN SHADES

A firmly woven fabric is the best choice for a Roman shade, and it should be lined. Roman shades are easy to make, but it is very important to transfer the measurements accurately at all stages to make sure that the shade hangs straight. Also, always position one of the rows of rings down the center, even if the shade is narrow.

C H E C K L I S T

Materials

fabric
lining
wooden rods
rings as required
cord
1 in (25 mm) wide touch-and-close fastener
screw eyes
cleat
general sewing equipment   page 134

Techniques

Measuring

For the amount of fabric, lining, dowel, and cord required, see page 90.

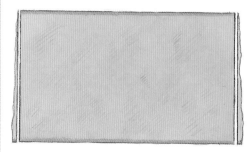

1 Make sure that the cut edges of the fabric and lining are straight and at right angles to the selvages. Trim off the selvages. Cut and if necessary join the fabric lengths and lining lengths with open seams.

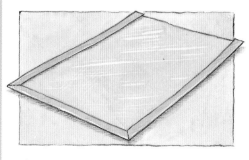

2 Turn 1 in (2.5 cm) to the wrong side on the sides and bottom of the main fabric and pin in place. Press the hems and form a miter in each bottom corner, removing pins.

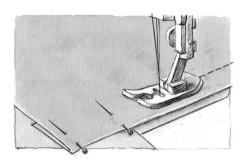

3 Re-pin the side and bottom hems on the right side and topstitch $\frac{5}{8}$ in (1.5 cm) from the folded edges, removing pins as you stitch.

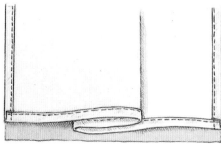

4 Turn $\frac{1}{2}$ in (1.2 cm) to the wrong side on the sides and bottom of the lining and pin in place. Press the hems and machine stitch, removing the pins as you stitch.

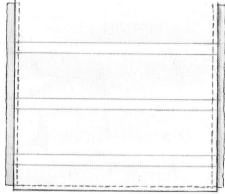

5 Lay the lining right side up on a flat surface and mark the stitching lines for the rod channels based on your measurements.

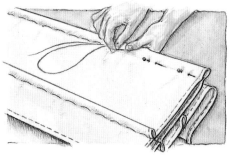

6 Bring the marked lines together to form the channels on the right side, and pin and baste them. Remove the pins. Machine stitch each channel and take out basting.

7 Lay the main fabric right side down and place the lining over it right side up. Align the raw edges at the top. The lining will be ½ in (1.2 cm) smaller than the main fabric at the sides and bottom.

8 Carefully smooth out the lining, making sure that it stays square to the main fabric. Pin the two fabrics together along the bottom edge of the lining and then alongside the stitching for the rod channels, working up from the bottom.

9 Baste along the bottom and along the stitching lines for the rod channels. Machine stitch along the rod channels only, making sure that the lines are horizontal and parallel to each other.

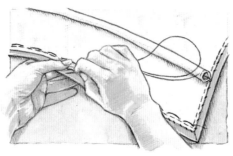

10 Pin the sides of the lining to the shade between the channels. Slipstitch the lining to the shade along the sides and bottom edge.

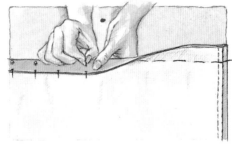

11 Baste the raw edges of the fabric and lining together across the top. Turn 1 in (2.5 cm) to the wrong side and pin. Machine stitch the "loop" side of fastener over the raw edges with zigzag stitch, removing pins as you stitch.

12 Insert a rod into each channel and stitch across the ends of each channel to hold the rods in place.

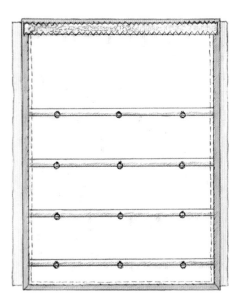

13 Position the cording rings on the folded edges of the channels 3 in (7.5 cm) in from each side and at intervals of approximately 12 in (30 cm) across the width of the shade. Stitch the rings in place.

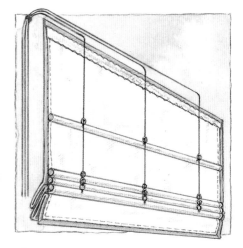

14 Cut the required number of lengths of cord, allowing enough for threading through the screw eyes and down the operating side when hanging the shade. Knot a length of cord firmly to each bottom ring, and then thread the cords through the vertical rows of rings. Hang the shade.

BALLOON SHADES

A balloon shade is a combination of a Roman shade and a festoon shade. It is flat at the top and ruched into swags at the bottom, and is made with extra width in the fabric, which allows inverted pleats to be formed and pressed.

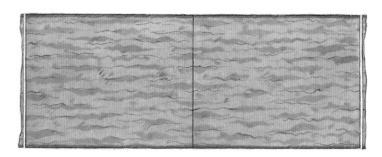

1 Cut the fabric and lining into drop lengths, based on your measurements. Trim off the selvages and join lengths with open seams, matching patterns if necessary.

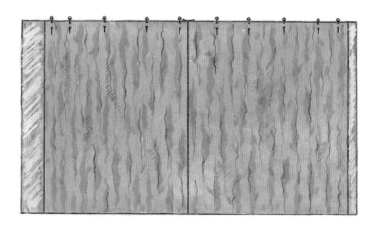

2 Lay the main fabric right side up and mark the spaces, pleats, and side allowances with pins, making sure that any seams will be under a pleat fold.

3 Cut off the surplus width on both the main fabric and lining, taking a further 2 in (5 cm) from each side of the lining. Remove the marker pins from the top of the main fabric. Mark the center of both the fabric and lining, top and bottom, with a pin.

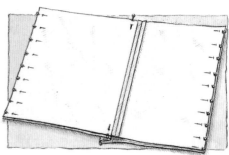

4 With right sides together, align the raw edges of the main fabric and lining at the sides and pin. Machine stitch $\frac{5}{8}$ in (1.5 cm) from the edges, removing pins as you stitch. Press the seam open.

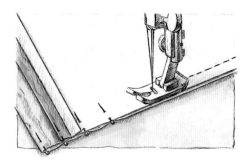

5 With the lining uppermost, match the center pins, leaving an equal margin of main fabric visible at each side. Pin the bottom edges together, and machine stitch $\frac{1}{2}$ in (1.2 cm) from the raw edges. Trim the corners. Remove the pins.

6 Turn right side out and press the sides, so that an equal amount of the main fabric shows at each side. Smooth out the shade right side up on a flat surface and baste the top raw edges together.

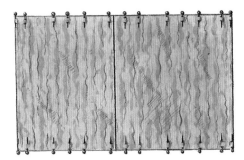

7 Check the pleat and space measurements on your plan and re-mark with pins along the top and opposite along the bottom. Form the pleats, pin them in place, then press along the fold lines.

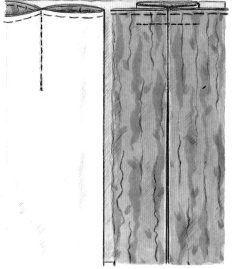

8 Machine stitch down the inside of each pleat for 4 in (10 cm) from the top. Re-press the pleats and then stitch straight across each one to secure them in place.

9 Turn under $\frac{5}{8}$ in (1.5 cm) to the wrong side along the top of the shade and pin. Machine the "loop" side of the fastener tape with zigzag stitch over the raw edge, removing pins as you stitch.

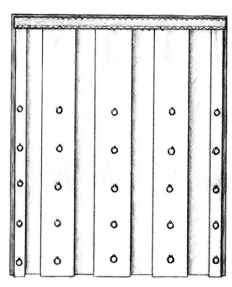

10 Position the cording rings along the center of each pleat, starting 2 in (5 cm) from the bottom and finishing 10 in (25 cm) from the fastener tape. Space the remainder approximately 6 in (15 cm) apart. Stitch the rings firmly in place through both the fabric and lining.

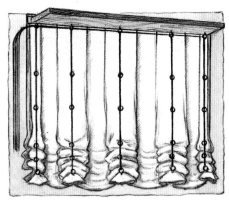

11 Knot a length of cord firmly to each bottom ring, and then thread the cords through the vertical rows of rings. Hang the shade.

To keep swags permanently ruched at desired height, raise the shade and tie or sew two or more of the rings together on each side of the vertical rows at the back.

FESTOON SHADES

A festoon shade is gathered across the top using a pencil-pleat heading tape, and when pulled up, it ruches upward, forming deep swags across the width of the shade. A ruffle added to the bottom and sides of the shade can give a luxurious and feminine look in a bedroom, while a ruffle across the bottom can contrast with other furnishings in the room.

C H E C K L I S T

Materials

Techniques

Measuring

For fabric, lining, fastener, ring, cord, and heading tape requirements, see page 93.

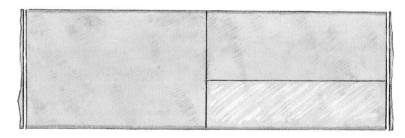

1 Cut the fabric and lining into drop lengths. Trim off the selvages and measure precisely the widths you require from your calculated measurements. Cut off the surplus.

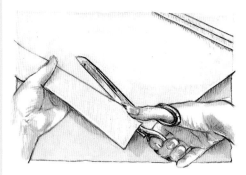

2 Join the fabric widths together with open seams, and do the same for the lining widths. Trim 2 in (5 cm) from both the side edges of the lining. Mark the center of each side edge with a pin.

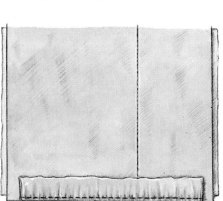

3 Make the ruffle and attach it to the bottom of the main fabric, placing the finished ends of the ruffle 1⅝ in (4 cm) from the side edges. Machine stitch in place ⅝ in (1.5 cm) from the raw edges.

4 Baste the ruffle up on the right side of the shade to keep it out of the way.

5 Place the fabric and lining right sides together (remember that the fabric is larger than the lining), align the side edges, pin and baste together. Remove the pins, machine stitch, and press the seam open.

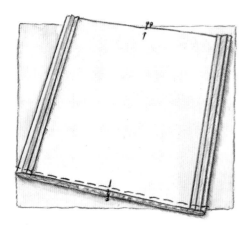

6 Matching the center marks, smooth out the lining and position it over the ruffle seam, leaving an equal margin of the main fabric visible at each side. Pin across the bottom of the shade, baste, and remove the pins.

7 Turn the shade over and machine stitch across the bottom, following the row of stitching from attaching the ruffle. Trim the seam and the corners.

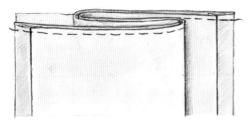

8 Turn the shade right side out and release the basting holding the ruffle. Baste the fabric and lining together across the top. Press the shade. Remove center pins.

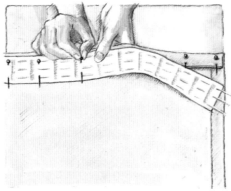

9 Turn under $\frac{5}{8}$ in (1.5 cm) to the wrong side at the top of the shade and attach the pencil-pleat contact heading tape with a straight machine stitch over the raw edges.

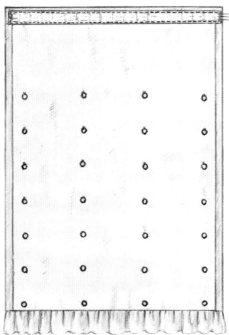

10 Position the cording rings starting 2 in (5 cm) from the ruffle seam and finishing 12 in (30 cm) from the heading tape. Space the remainder approximately 8 in (20 cm) apart. The outside rows should start 2 in (5 cm) from the side edges.

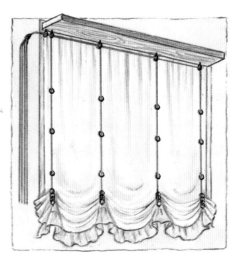

11 Stitch the rings firmly in place through both the fabric and lining. Knot a length of cord firmly to each bottom ring, and then thread a cord through each vertical row of rings. Hang the shade.

PILLOWS

Pillows can be made in a variety of shapes and sizes, and provide added comfort as well as being a decorative feature which can link the colors in a room. As only a small amount of fabric is required, it is possible to experiment with different types of fabrics and colors and to use remnants from other projects. Instructions are given for making heart-shaped, round, square, and box-shaped pillows, and bolsters, with suggestions for methods of fastenings and trimmings.

SELF-BORDERED PILLOW

This style of pillow would look good in a living room or bedroom. It is easy to make as the border is included with the cover when cutting out, and touch-and-close fastener is used. Instructions are given for a standard-size pillow form size. For non-standard sizes, see Measuring.

CHECK LIST

Materials

16 in (40 cm) pillow form
24 in (60 cm) of 48 in (122 cm) wide fabric
12 in (30 cm) touch-and-close fastener
general sewing equipment   page 134

Techniques

cutting	page 136
basting	page 138
zigzag stitch	page 141
machine stitching	page 140
pressing	page 137
attaching touch-and-close tape	page 146

Measuring

To calculate the amount of fabric required for a non-standard pillow, measure the pillow form as shown, adding 4 in (10 cm) to each measurement.

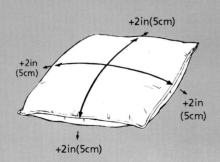

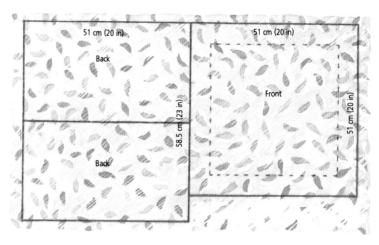

1 Lay the fabric right side down and mark the cutting lines for one front piece and two back pieces with tailor's chalk. Cut out the pieces.

2 Turn 1 in (2.5 cm) to the wrong side along the center edges of one back piece and pin. Baste the hem, remove the pins, and finish the raw edge with zigzag stitch. Repeat with second back piece. Press the hems.

3 Stitch the hook side of the touch-and-close fastener to the right side of one back piece, positioning it an equal distance from each end.

4 Stitch the loop side to the wrong side of the other back piece, making sure the two sides will be aligned when fastened.

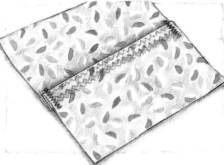

5 With the touch-and-close strips fastened, machine stitch across the ends of the opening.

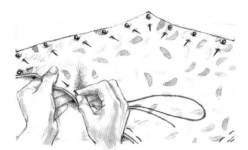

6 Place the front and back of the cover right sides together and pin around all four sides. Baste around the four sides and remove the pins. Machine stitch all around $\frac{1}{2}$ in (1.3 cm) from the raw edges.

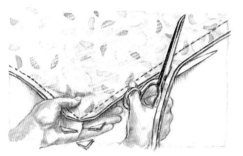

7 Trim the seam close to the stitching, and clip across the corners. Turn the cover right side out and press.

8 With the back of the pillow-cover fastened, mark a stitching line with tailor's chalk around all four sides 2 in (5 cm) from the outer edges. Topstitch along the line and remove pins. Press the cover and insert the cushion pad.

Self-bordered pillows are attractive and easy to sew. Make them all in the same fabric to co ordinate with other furnishings in the room or, if you have plain upholstery, make each pillow in a different color for maximum impact.

ROUND PIPED PILLOW

The throw pillow shown here is trimmed with piping. You could attach a ruffle to coordinate with the curtains or upholstery. Instructions are based on a standard-size pillow form, for a non-standard size, see Measuring.

Measuring

Measure the diameter of the pillow form, and make a pattern from a square piece of paper 2 in (5 cm) larger than this measurement. For a non-standard size pillow, measure the outside circumference of the pillow form which includes ⅜ in (1 cm) seam allowance.

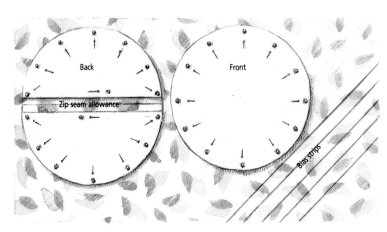

1 Pin the circle patterns to the fabric, marking the zipper seam allowance directly on the material.

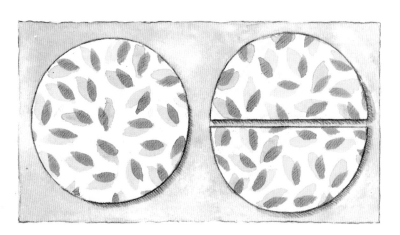

2 Cut out the fabric for the pillow cover, cutting along the zipper seam on the back piece. Cut bias strips for the piping.

3 To join the back pieces, place them right sides together. Pin them along the zipper seam, then baste them together ⅝ in (1.5 cm) from the raw edges. Remove pins.

4 Machine stitch along the zipper seam for 2 in (5 cm) in from each side. Machine baste the center section and press seams open. Insert the zipper.

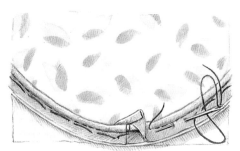

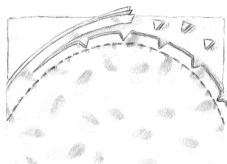

5 Join the bias strips for piping to make a length equal to the circumference of the pillow plus 1 in (2.5 cm). Make the piping and attach to the front cover piece. Join the ends of the piping.

8 Trim the seam and notch all around, being careful not to cut into the stitching.

9 Turn the cover right sides out, press and insert the pillow form. Close zipper.

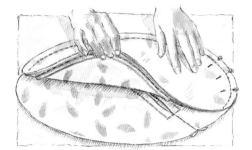

6 With the zipper partly open, place the front and back pieces right sides together, and pin them all around the edge. Baste all around and remove the pins.

7 With the front piece on top, machine stitch all around, following the line of stitching from applying the piping.

Piping can be used on a pillow to contrast with the main color or to tone with a patterned fabric. Piping also helps to define the shape of a pillow, especially if there are several pillows stacked together.

HEART-SHAPED PILLOW

This an ideal throw pillow for a romantic room style. For an extra-special look, use contrasting ribbon to trim the finished cover, either hand stitching tiny bows or roses to the front, or threading a narrow length of ribbon through an eyelet ruffle. Because of its shape, it is necessary to make the pillow form yourself.

CHECK LIST

Materials

graph paper for paper pattern – see
   template   page 156
pillow form: 20 in (50 cm) of 36 in (90 cm) wide
   thin cotton fabric
   medium-sized bag of synthetic stuffing
pillow cover: 20 in (50 cm) of 36 in (90 cm) wide
   fabric
   2¼ yds (2 m) of 2⅜ in (6 cm) wide eyelet lace trim
   3 snaps
general sewing equipment   page 138

Techniques

cutting	page 136
basting	page 138
machine stitching	page 140
slipstitch	page 139
seams	page 142
zigzag stitch	page 141
top stitch	page 141
ruffles and gathering	page 150
attaching snaps	page 147
pressing	page 137

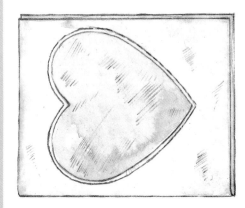

1 To make the pillow form, cut out two pieces from the thin cotton fabric using the pattern on page 154. Add ⅜ in (1 cm) all around. With right sides facing, pin, then baste the two pieces together and remove pins.

2 Machine stitch ½ in (1.3 cm) from the raw edges, leaving a 4 in (10 cm) opening on one side.

3 Trim the seam. Notch without cutting too close to the stitching, and snip where the shape dips inward. Turn the cover right side out. Stuff it and slipstitch the gap to close.

4 To make the cover, cut out one piece of fabric to the exact size of the pattern for the front.

5 For the back, cut the pattern into two pieces and place them on the fabric with a gap of 3 in (7.5 cm) between them for the fastening. Cut out the two pieces.

6 To make the ruffle, join the ends of the eyelet lace trim with a narrow seam. Zigzag stitch both the edges together to finish, and press to one side.

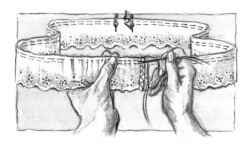

7 Find the point halfway around the lace from the seam and mark it with a tailor's tack. Gather the ruffle along the raw edge, breaking off the threads at seam and tailor's tack.

8 Position the ruffle on the front piece of the cover, with right sides together and raw edges even. Place the ruffle seam at the top and the tailor's tack mark at the bottom of the heart.

9 Pin the ruffle in place, even out the gathers, baste, and machine ½ in (1.3 cm) from raw edges. Baste down the outer edges of the ruffle to right side of front.

10 To prepare the back, turn under 1 in (2.5 cm) to the wrong side on the cut edges of the opening and zigzag stitch to finish.

11 Overlap the zigzagged edges by 1 in (2.5 cm) and topstitch 2 in (5 cm) in from each side. Position and attach snaps and fasten them. The back should now be the same size as the front.

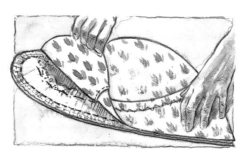

12 Place the back over the front, with right sides together, and raw edges even. Pin, then baste together, and remove the pins. Machine stitch with the front on top to follow the ruffle stitching line.

13 Trim the seam, notch around the curves and snip toward the dip. Turn the cover right side out and remove the basting to release the lace trim. Press the cover and insert the pillow form.

Heart-shaped pillows can be made in a pretty flowered fabric and trimmed with lace for a romantic bedroom look. Add a personal touch with ribbon roses and bows.

SQUARE BOX CUSHION

Box cushions are ideal for coordinating garden furniture and window seats.

CHECK LIST

Materials

heavyweight upholstery fabric – see Measuring
piping cord (pre-shrink before use)
zipper, 6 in (15 cm) longer than width of back of pillow
box-shaped latex or foam pad
general sewing equipment   page 134

Techniques

cutting   page 136
basting   page 138
machine stitching   page 140
making piping   page 149
inserting a zipper   page 147

Measuring

Following the diagram, measure the cushion form to to calculate the amount of fabric required.
Top and bottom pieces – measure the length (A to B) and width (C to D) of the form (they will be the same if it is truly square) and add 1¼ in (3 cm) for seam allowances for both measurements.
Front welt – measure the length (E to F) and the depth (G to H) and add 1¼ in (3 cm) to both measurements.
Side welt – measure the length (E to F) and deduct 1¾ in (4.5 cm). Measure the depth (G to H) and add 1¼ in (3 cm).
Back welt – measure the length (E to F) add 7¼ in (18 cm). Measure the depth (G to H) and add 2¼ in (6 cm).

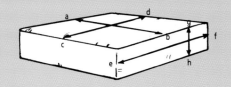

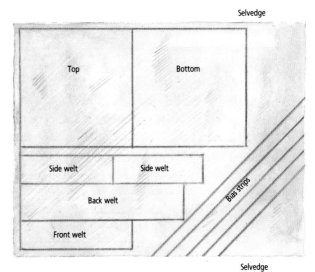

1 Using your measurements, mark the cutting lines for the top, bottom, and welt pieces of the cushion, following the cutting plan. Cut out the pieces and bias strips for the piping.

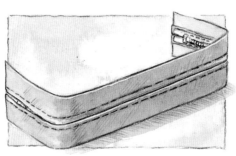

2 Cut the back welt piece in half lengthwise. Insert the zipper.

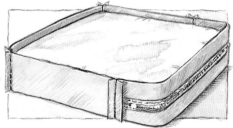

4 Before stitching, insert cushion pad into joined welt to check for a snug fit. Baste along pinned seams ⅝ in (1.5 cm) from the raw edges, remove the pins, and stitch. Press the seams open.

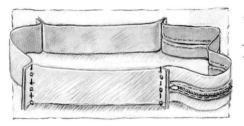

3 With right sides together, pin side welt pieces to each end of the back piece. Then pin the other ends of the side welt pieces to each end of the front welt piece.

5 Make enough piping to go around the top and bottom pieces of the cushion cover, and apply them to each piece, snipping each corner of the piping "skirt."

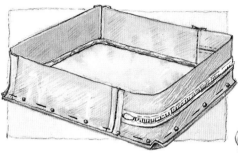

6 With right sides together and corners matching, pin the welt to the top piece on all four sides.

Cover box cushions in lively bold fabrics which contrast with throw pillows. For a window seat, cover in the same fabric as the curtains. As this cushion is for the seat of a chair, it needs to fit snugly.

9 Turn the cover right side out, insert the cushion pad and close the zipper.

7 Baste along the line of piping stitching, remove the pins, and stitch close to the basting.

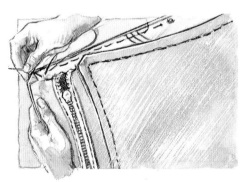

8 With the zipper partly open, attach the bottom piece to the welt in the same way. Trim the seams, snip into seam allowances of the welt, and cut across the corners.

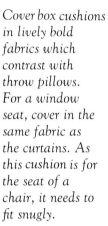

BOLSTER WITH TIES

Bolsters are firm pillows for use on beds and sofas, where a pair is placed at each end. They are cylindrical in shape, made from a block of foam or a very firmly stuffed fabric roll with round ends. Tube-like covers are very easy and quick to make, and the ends can be trimmed with tassels, ribbon, or buttons.

C H E C K   L I S T

Materials

bolster form
lightweight fabric – see Measuring
general sewing equipment   page 134

Techniques

cutting	page 136
pressing	page 137
machine stitching	page 140
making ties	page 146

Measuring

Measure the length of the bolster and the diameter of one end and add 2¼ in (6 cm). Measure the circumference and add 1¼ in (3 cm).

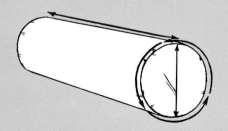

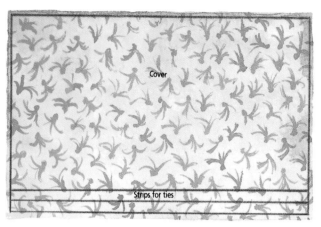

1 Cut out the fabric required for the bolster cover. From the remaining fabric, cut two strips 1⅝ in (4 cm) wide by 48 in (1.2 m.

2 With right sides facing and raw edges even, pin the long edges together. Machine stitch ⅝ in (1.5 cm) from the raw edges. Press the seam open and turn right side out.

4 Unpick a few of the seam stitches on the right side of the bolster at the hem end. Attach a safety pin to one end of fabric tie, insert into the opening, and thread the strips through the hem casing. Repeat at the other end.

3 Turn ⅜ in (1 cm) to the wrong side at one end, pin and press. Turn a further ¾ in (2 cm) to make a double hem, pin and machine stitch. Remove the pins. Press and repeat at other end of fabric tube. Make the fabric ties.

5 Insert the bolster into the cover. It should be a snug fit with an even amount of fabric at each end. Pull up the fabric ties to gather the ends. Tie into bows.

MAKING TASSELS

Tassels can be used to co-ordinate colors and fabrics. Any material is suitable, and colors and textures can be mixed for added contrast. Bold tassels can be made from bundles of yarn, rolled-up pleated fabrics, or strips of leather.

1 Cut two pieces of cardboard the length of the tassel. Wind the yarn around the two pieces of board placed together. With two lengths of yarn tie one loop through the top of the yarn and thread another piece through this loop several times.

2 At the opposite end cut the yarn between the cards.

3 Bind tassel about ½ in (15 mm) from the top, secure the yarn, and leave enough yarn for attaching the tassel.

Tassels, colored buttons, rosettes, and separate fabric ends can all be added to bolster pillows to help create a coordinated look. Buy or make huge rosettes in the same or toning fabric, add a self-covered or contrasting button, or make separate ends in a complementary color that coordinates with other colors in the room.

BED LINEN

Items of bed linen are very easy to make, as most of the sewing consists of stitching straight lines. Instructions in this section give the simplest way to achieve a good professional finish. Easy-care mix-and-match poly/cotton sheeting can be used for most of the items, including a choice of two methods for making pillowcases, a box-springs base valance, and a duvet cover made from just stitching two pieces together. The bed throw is the easiest way of giving a fully co-ordinated look to a bedroom.

PLAIN PILLOWCASE

A standard pillowcase is made from one piece of fabric which can match or contrast with existing bed linen. Larger pillows, say for a teenager's bedroom, can be made in the same way using any practical, easy-to-wash material.

C H E C K L I S T

Materials

polyester/cotton sheeting – see Measuring	
general sewing equipment	page 134

Techniques

cutting	page 136
basting	page 138
machine stitching	page 140
French seam	page 143
pressing	page 137

Measuring

As sizes vary, it is important to measure the pillow in order to calculate the amount of fabric required. Following the diagram, measure the length from A to B, double it, and add 9 in (23 cm) for flap and hem allowance. Measure the width from C to D and add 3 cm (1¼ in) for seams.

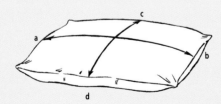

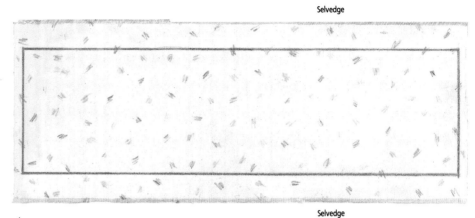

Selvedge

Selvedge

1 Cut a piece of fabric on the straight grain to the required length and width.

2 Make a double hem across one short end of the piece of fabric by turning over ¼ in (6 mm) to the wrong side twice, and pin in place. Baste the hem, remove the pins, and machine stitch.

3 At the opposite short end of the piece of fabric, turn 2¼ in (6 cm) to the wrong side and press the fold.

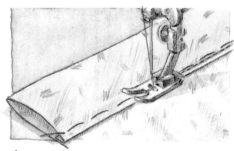

4 Turn the raw edge under ¼ in (6 mm) and pin in place. Baste the hem, remove the pins, and machine stitch close to the basting.

5 Lay the piece of fabric right side down. Fold over the end with the narrow hem 6¼ in (16 cm) and pin in place. Press the fold and remove the pins.

6 Fold the piece of fabric in half with the wrong sides together and the short ends aligned so the flap is enclosed. Pin the sides together, and then baste along each side. Remove pins.

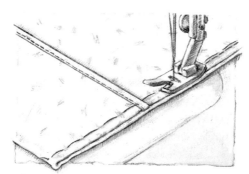

8 Turn the pillowcase inside out and baste along each side as for a French seam. Machine stitch and remove basting.

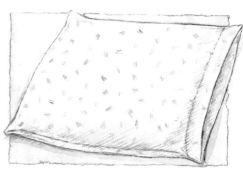

9 Turn the pillowcase right side out and press it to finish.

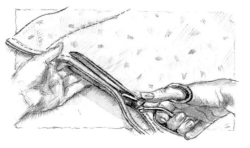

7 Machine stitch through all layers along each side $\frac{1}{4}$ in (6 mm) from the raw edges. Remove basting and trim side seams to $\frac{1}{8}$ in (3 mm).

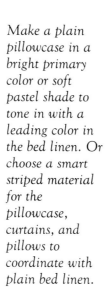

Make a plain pillowcase in a bright primary color or soft pastel shade to tone in with a leading color in the bed linen. Or choose a smart striped material for the pillowcase, curtains, and pillows to coordinate with plain bed linen.

RUFFLED PILLOWCASE

If you want to add a coordinating or contrasting ruffle to a pillowcase, this method, which consists of three pieces of fabric, is best.

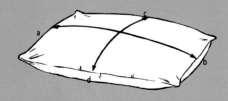

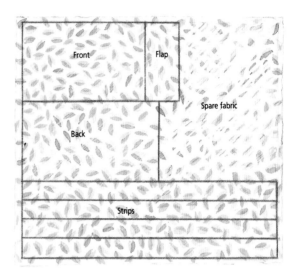

1 Lay the fabric right side down and mark out the cutting lines for the front, back, flap, and ruffle pieces on it with tailor's chalk, based on your measurements. Cut out the pieces.

2 Find the center on each side of the front piece and mark with tailor's tacks.

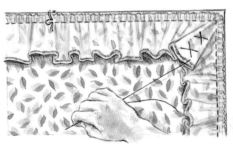

3 Join strips to make the ruffle, mark in four equal lengths with tailor's tacks and attach it to the front piece of the pillowcase, matching the tailor's tacks. Baste the corners of the ruffle to the front piece.

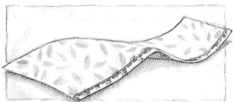

4 Make a double hem on one long side of the flap piece by turning ¼ in (6 mm) to the wrong side twice, and pin in place. Baste the hem, remove the pins, and machine stitch close to the basting.

5 Place the flap piece over one end of the front piece with the right sides together and the raw edges aligned. Pin in place.

6 Baste the flap and front pieces together across the end. Remove the pins. Machine stitch through all layers close to the basting.

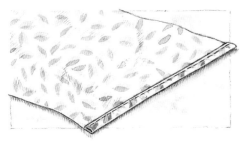

7 Make a double hem across one of the short ends of the back piece by turning ⅝ in (1.5 cm) to the wrong side twice, and pin in place. Baste the hem, remove the pins, and machine stitch close to the basting.

8 Open out the flap. Place the back piece over the front piece with the right sides together, and with the hemmed end of the back aligned with the flap seam. Pin in place, and then baste through all layers. Remove the pins.

9 Replace the flap over the back piece. Baste through all the layers of fabric along both long sides of the pillowcase and across the end opposite the flap.

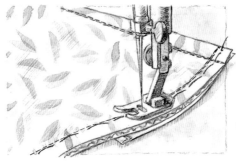

10 Turn the assembled pillowcase over, and, following the ruffle stitching line, machine stitch ⅝ in (1.5 cm) in from the raw edges along both long sides and across the end opposite the flap.

Ruffled pillowcases help to give a romantic look to a bedroom. The ruffle can be the same colour as the main pillow fabric, or choose a ruffle in a contrasting colour which echoes the fabric used for the curtains, bed valance or duvet cover.

11 Work a second row of machine stitching on the outside of the first row ¼ in (6 mm) away from it, around all four sides. Trim the seam close to the stitching and finish with zigzag stitch.

12 Turn the pillowcase right side out. Remove the basting stitches from the flap end and in the corners to release the ruffle, and press the pillowcase.

DUVET COVER

Duvet covers are very easy to make because they are made from just two pieces of fabric sewn together. You could use the same fabric for both sides, or choose two contrasting fabrics for a reversible duvet. Gripper-tape is used to close the opening at the bottom.

Measuring

Following the diagram, measure the length of the comforter from A to B and add 2⅝ in (6.5 cm) for hems, then double this measurement. Measure the width from C to D and add 1¼ in (3 cm) for seams.

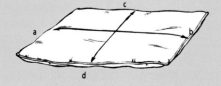

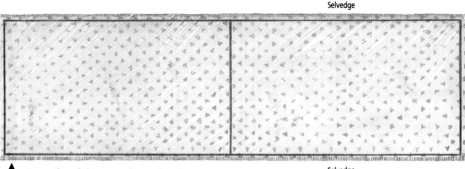

Selvedge

Selvedge

1 Lay the fabric right side down and mark the cutting lines for the two pieces of fabric with tailor's chalk. Cut out the two pieces.

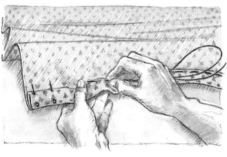

2 Make a double hem across one end of each piece by turning 1 in (2.5 cm) to the wrong side twice, and pin in place. Baste the hem and remove the pins. Machine stitch close to the basting, and then press the hems.

3 Place the two pieces of fabric with the right sides together and the hemmed edges aligned. Pin the two pieces together on the inside edge of the hem, stitching at a distance of 12 in (30 cm) in from each side.

4 Baste along each line of pins, and then remove the pins. Machine stitch close to the basting.

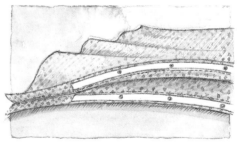

5 Unfasten the strip of gripper-tape and position each part with one long edge close to the hem stitching line across the opening. Check that the press snaps match for fastening, and center the tape so that a snap is at an equal distance from each side of the opening.

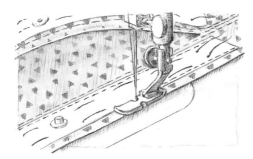

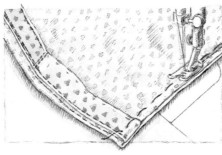

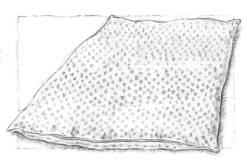

6 Machine stitch the tape in place using a zipper foot so that you can stitch in a straight line past the snaps. Fasten the snaps.

9 Turn the cover inside out and machine stitch around the three sides $\frac{1}{4}$ in (6 mm) in from folded edges, enclosing the raw edges.

10 Turn the cover right sides out again and press. As an alternative fastening for the duvet cover, you could use buttons or tied bows.

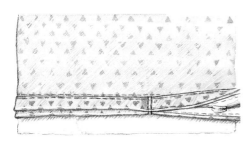

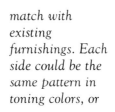

7 At each end of the opening, machine stitch down the hem from the folded edge to the stitching line to enclose the raw edges of the gripper-tape. Make a second line of the stitching close to the first and fasten off securely.

A reversible duvet cover is the easiest way to create a fully coordinated look that can mix and match with existing furnishings. Each side could be the same pattern in toning colors, or choose two differently-patterned fabrics in complementary colors.

8 Turn the cover right sides out. Pin down both the sides and top of the cover, then baste and remove the pins. Machine stitch $\frac{1}{4}$ in (6 mm) from the raw edges. Trim the seam to $\frac{1}{8}$ in (3 mm).

BED VALANCE

A bed valance covers the box springs neatly and can coordinate either with the bedding or with other furnishings in the room such as curtains. If this is your first attempt at making a large item, choose easy-to-handle sheeting for your fabric.

CHECK LIST

Materials

fabric – see Measuring	
general sewing equipment	page 134
small plate	

Techniques

cutting	page 136
French seam	page 143
basting	page 138
machine stitching	page 140
pressing	page 137
tailor's tacks	page 138

Measuring

Main panel – measure the length from A to B and add 1⅜ in (3.5 cm) for seam allowances. Measure the width from C to D and add 1¼ in (3 cm).
Valance – measure the depth from E to F and add 1 in (2.5 cm). For the length, calculate 3 times the length (A to B) plus 1½ times the width (C to D). Add 1½ in (4 cm).

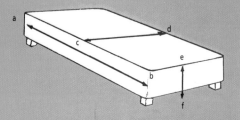

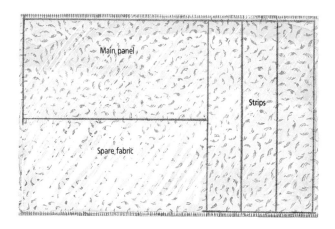

1 Based on the measurements of the bed, lay the fabric right side down and mark the cutting lines for the pieces required with tailor's chalk.

2 Cut out the main panel. Form a curve on each of the bottom corners by placing a small plate across the corner and drawing around it with tailor's chalk.

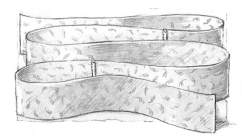

3 Cut out the fabric strips to make the required length for the valance, and join them into one continuous strip with French seams.

4 Make a double hem along one long edge of the valance strip by turning ⅜ in (1 cm) to the wrong side twice. Pin in place, baste the hem, and remove pins. Machine stitch close to the basting. Press the hem.

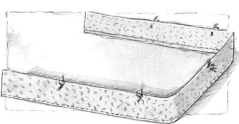

5 Divide the valance strip into six equal sections using a tape-measure, or by folding the valance. Mark the divisions with tailor's tacks.

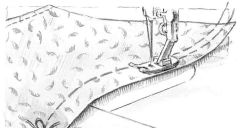

6 With the right side up, work two rows of machine stitching along the raw edge ⅝ in (1.5 cm) and ⅜ in (1 cm) from the edge. Use the longest stitch setting, and break off thread at each tailor's tack.

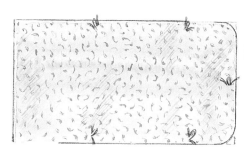

7 Divide the main panel into six equal sections around the sides and bottom edge, and mark with tailor's tacks. Gather the valance and with right sides facing, pin and baste it to the main panel, as for a ruffle.

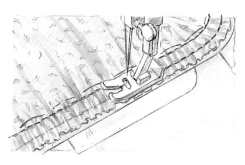

8 Machine stitch the valance to the main panel ⅝ in (1.5 cm) in from the raw edges. Work another row of machine stitching using the second row of gathering as a guide.

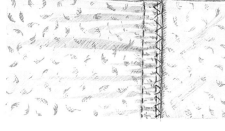

9 Trim the seam close to the second row of stitching and stitch with a zigzag stitch to finish. Press the seam toward the main panel.

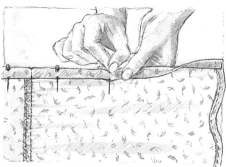

10 Make a double hem across the straight end of the valance strip and the main panel by turning ⅜ in (1 cm) to the wrong side twice, and pin in place.

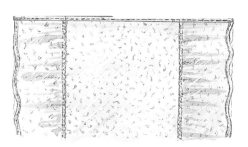

11 Baste across the top hem, remove the pins, and machine stitch close to the basting.

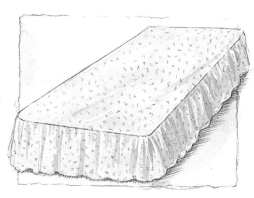

12 Press the valance to finish and spread over the bed with the ruffled short edge at the foot of the bed.

A gathered bed valance hides the base of the bed and can be made in a pretty fabric that coordinates with a frilled pillowcase or duvet cover. For a more striking look, use a bold, solid fabric that matches the sheets or duvet.

BED THROW

A bed throw covers all the bedding and is the best way to coordinate a bedroom, especially if it matches the curtains. This throw is reversible.

CHECK LIST

Materials

two coordinated fabrics – see Measuring	
general sewing equipment	page 134
pencil	
string	

Techniques

cutting	page 136
pressing	page 137
basting	page 138
machine stitching	page 140
slipstitch	page 139

Measuring

Following the diagram, measure the bed (fully made up), to calculate the size of a floor-length bedspread. You will need equal amounts of the main fabric and the contrasting lining fabric. Measure the length from A to B, and add 10 in (25 cm) to allow for tucking in under the pillows. Measure the width from C to D. Add 3⅝ in (9 cm) for seam allowances when the fabric is joined.

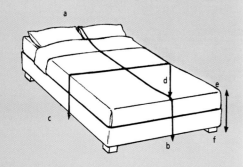

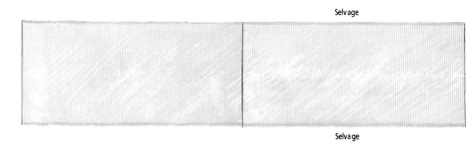

Selvage

Selvage

1 Lay one fabric right side down and mark the cutting lines for the two lengths required, based on the measurements of the bed. Make sure that any pattern matches. Cut out the two pieces.

2 Trim the selvage edges from the sides of both lengths, and cut one length in half lengthwise. Place the half-widths one on each side of the full width, matching the pattern if necessary.

3 Place the full width and one half-width right sides together and pin down the long edge. Baste pieces together, remove the pins, and machine stitch ⅝ in (1.5 cm) from the raw edges. Repeat on the other side.

4 To round off the corners at the bottom of the bedspread, measure the overhang from the top of the bed to the floor (E to F) and add ⅝ in (1.5 cm). Using the measurement, mark a square in each corner with tailor's chalk.

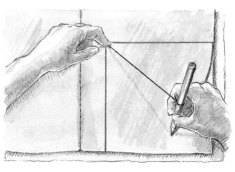

5 Take a pencil tied to a piece of string and hold the string on the inner corner of the square. Using one side of the square as the radius, draw an arc across the corner. Repeat on the other corner.

6 Cut off the two bottom corners of the bedspread carefully along the curved pencil line. Repeat instructions 2–7 to prepare the second fabric. Press all seams open.

9 Trim the seams and top corners. Notch the curved corners. Remove all the basting.

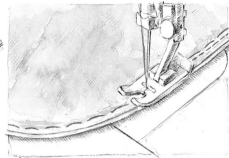

11 With the basting still in place, machine stitch around the edge of the bedspread using a medium-to-long stitch.

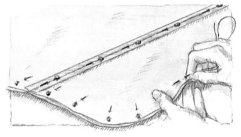

7 Lay the prepared fabrics right sides together, aligning the seams and raw edges. Pin and then baste the seams and edges together.

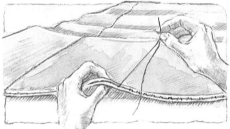

10 Turn the bedspread right side out and slipstitch across the opening to close it. Baste all around the edge of the bedspread, making sure that the seam is right on the edge, and press.

12 Remove the basting and give the bedspread a final press.

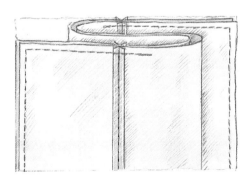

8 Machine stitch around the outside edges, leaving an opening of 36 in (90 cm) along the top.

A throw-over cover is quick and easy to make, and adds instant focus to the bedroom. For a strong statement use a bold, ethnic design in vivid colors. For a softer look use a flowered fabric that contrasts with plain bed linen.

TABLE LINEN

Color coordinated table linen made to match china as well as furnishings and decor creates an impressive and harmonious dining room setting. This section gives easy step-by-step instructions on how to make all the items required for a complete table arrangement: napkins, placemats, and a roll holder. As table linen is so quick and easy, you can make a suitable setting for any occasion, from a children's birthday party using a bright and lively fabric, to a wedding reception requiring a fine damask material.

RECTANGULAR TABLECLOTH

From a children's party to a wedding anniversary, the perfect table setting begins with the tablecloth. This rectangular cloth, which has a hem corded with crochet cotton, is easy to make and can be used to match existing furnishings.

C H E C K   L I S T

Materials

fabric see Measuring
mercerized crochet cotton
general sewing equipment   page 134

Techniques

cutting	page 136
pressing	page 137
mitering	page 144
zigzag stitch	page 141

Measuring

Following the diagram, measure the table to calculate the amount of fabric required. Measure from A to B and then C to D. Add 20 in (50 cm) to both measurements for overhang and hem allowance.

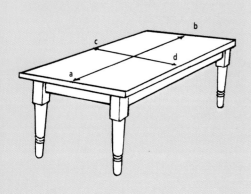

1 Lay the fabric right side down and mark the cutting lines for the size required with tailor's chalk, based on your measurements. Cut out the fabric.

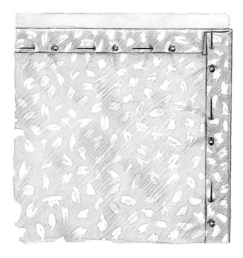

2 Turn under a hem of 1 in (2.5 cm) to the wrong side on all four edges of the fabric and pin it in place. Press the hem and remove the pins.

3 Turn under a further 1 in (2.5 cm) to form a double hem and pin in place. Press the hem again.

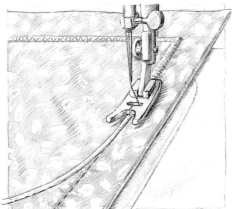

4 Miter the corners. Baste the hem in place, and then machine stitch close to the basting.

5 With right side up, lay a single strand of crochet cotton over the hem stitching. Using a zigzag stitch and matching thread, machine stitch over the croche cotton to form a corded hem, butting ends together where they join.

6 Press the tablecloth. To make coordinated placemats and napkins, see the box below.

PLACEMATS AND NAPKINS

Rectangular placemats can be made using the same method as for the tablecloth. A piece of fabric 14×20 in (35×50 cm) will give a finished size of 12×18 in (30×45 cm) if a double turn of $\frac{3}{8}$ in (1 cm) is used for the hems.

Napkins are generally square and range from 12 in (30 cm) for luncheon size, to 24 in (60 cm) for a formal dinner. The average size for general use is usually between 18 in (45 cm) and 20 in (50 cm) square.

Matching placemats and napkins can be made to co-ordinate with a tablecloth or can be made in a contrasting fabric to add interest. Buy extra fabric when making the kitchen or dining room curtains to achieve a truly co ordinated room and table.

ROUND TABLECLOTH

For a small round side table make a floor-length tablecloth with a shorter cloth over it. For a dining table, the cloth should be lap height. If the fabric needs joining to fit a large table, stitch equal-size strips to each side of a full-width central panel.

CHECKLIST

Materials

paper for pattern	
fabric	see below
general sewing equipment	page 134

Techniques

patterns	page 154
cutting out	page 136
machine stitching	page 140
basting	page 138
pressing	page 137

Measuring

Following the diagram, measure the table to calculate the amount of fabric required. Measure the diameter from A to B and the depth of the required overhang from C to D. Double the overhang measurement and add ¾ in (2 cm) hem allowance to give the size for a square of fabric.

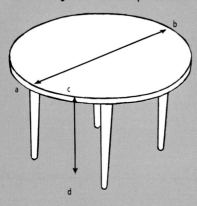

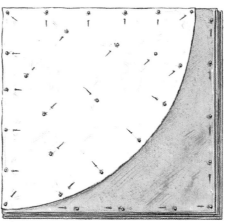

1 Fold the fabric in four and pin to secure the layers. Cut a piece of paper the same size as the folded fabric with an arc drawn across a corner to form a circle. Pin this pattern to the fabric and cut through all layers.

2 Machine stitch all around the circle of fabric, ⅝ in (1.5 cm) from the raw edge. Using the stitching line as a guide, press the edge of the fabric to the wrong side.

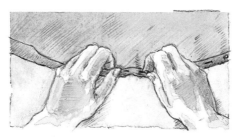

3 Turn under the raw edge to the pressed fold line to make a double hem and pin in place. Baste the hem, remove the pins, and then press.

4 Machine stitch all around the hem on the fold line and press it again. The double pressing helps to give a professional finish.

5 For a stylish finish, add a contrasting or coordinating overlay. A lace overlay on a solid-color fabric adds an attractive touch.

OVERLAY

To make a round overlay for the tablecloth, follow the same instructions, measuring a depth of about one-third of the top-to-floor measurement. This will be easier to judge if you make the full-length cloth first. A square lace cloth also looks attractive.

QUILTED PLACEMATS

Quilted placemats, which consist of a layer of batting covered with fabric, can be made to coordinate with the rest of the table linen. To quilt the mat, rows of stitching are machined or hand-sewn through all the layers.

CHECK LIST

Materials (for each placemat)

paper for pattern

1 piece each of 2 coordinated fabrics – 12 × 18 in (30 × 45 cm)

1 piece medium-weight batting 12 × 18 in (30 × 45 cm)

approximately 1⅝ yd (1.4 m) of 1 in (2.5 cm) wide bias binding (or make your own, see page 148)

general sewing equipment   page 134

Techniques

cutting	page 136
basting	page 138
machine stitching	page 140
slipstitch	page 139

Making the pattern

Fold a piece of paper measuring 12 × 18 in (30 × 45 cm) into four. Mark with pencil 6 in (15 cm) in from point A, and draw an arc to make an oval. Cut out the pattern.

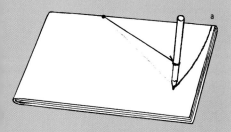

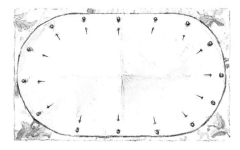

1 For each placemat, cut out one piece of each coordinated fabric and one piece of batting using the paper pattern.

2 Place the batting on the wrong side of the contrasting fabric, and lay the main fabric right side up over the batting. Baste the three layers together, working from the center outward.

3 Machine stitch the layers together using a large stitch setting, either following a design on the fabric or working freehand without creating any particular design.

4 Fold over ⅜ in (1 cm) to the wrong side of one end of the bias binding. Place the bias binding right side down on the right side of the main fabric, with raw edges even and pin in place.

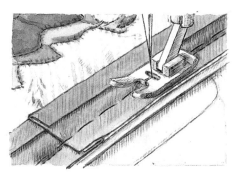

5 Baste the bias binding in place and remove the pins. Machine stitch ⅜ in (1 cm) from the raw edges. Fold the bias binding over to the contrasting fabric side. Slipstitch it neatly along the machine stitching and where it meets.

6 Lightly press the binding, but do not press the quilting.

ROLL HOLDER

A roll holder that matches the tablecloth or napkins provides an attractive centerpiece. This one is made from three circles of fabric laid on top of each other with matching ribbons for ties.

C H E C K L I S T

Materials

paper for pattern
20 in (50 cm) of 2 coordinated fabrics
20 in (50 cm) iron-on interfacing
3¼ yds (3 m) cotton lace trim
2¼ yds (2 m) wide ribbon
general sewing equipment   page 134

Techniques

cutting   page 136
pressing   page 137
basting   page 138
machine stitching   page 140
slipstitch   page 139
zigzag stitch   page 141

Making the pattern

Make a pattern by folding a 12 in (30 cm) square piece of paper into four. Draw an arc across a corner to make a circle and cut out the pattern. Divide it into twelve equal segments and mark them in pencil.

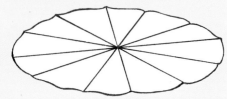

1 Cut out three circles from each fabric, and three from the interfacing, using the paper pattern. Position the pieces of interfacing on the wrong sides of the main fabric circles and press in place.

2 Pin the lace trim to the right sides all around the edges of the main fabric circles. Baste the lace trim in place, remove the pins, and machine stitch in position.

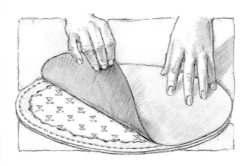

3 Place the contrasting fabric circles over the trimmed circles with right sides facing, and pin them together.

4 Baste all around ⅜ in (1 cm) from the raw edges, and remove the pins. Machine stitch following the stitching from applying the lace, leaving a 4 in (10 cm) opening for turning right side out.

5 Trim the seams and notch all around the edge of each circle. Turn the circles right sides out and slipstitch the gap closed. Press each circle.

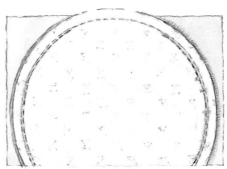

6 Place the paper pattern on the contrasting side of one of the circles and transfer every other line, to give six segments, using tailor's chalk.

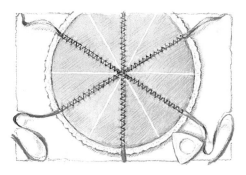

7 Cut the ribbon into three equal pieces. Center them over the chalk lines and stitch them down with zigzag stitch. Place the pattern over this circle again, and mark the lines between the ribbon lines.

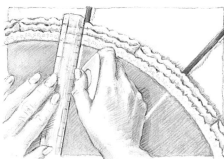

10 Turn the joined circles over, and place the third circle, with the contrasting fabric uppermost, on top. Mark lines from the points where the ribbons meet the edge of the circle, toward the center, with tailor's chalk.

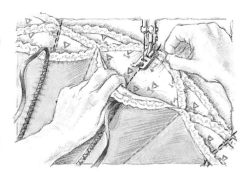

12 Machine stitch on the basting lines, working with the middle circle uppermost and from the outer edge of the circle toward the center.

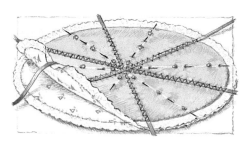

8 Place the circle with the ribbons uppermost over the main fabric side of a second circle. Pin them together along the chalk lines, working from the center out. Baste along the lines and remove the pins.

11 Pin along the lines for 3 in (7.5 cm) through the top and middle circles *only*. Baste along the lines and remove the pins.

13 Bring the opposite ribbons together and tie them in bows. Insert the roll holder in a basket and open up the pockets.

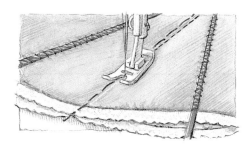

9 Machine stitch close to the basting, starting at the center for each line of stitching and working outward. Remove basting.

A bread roll holder is not only an eye-catching alternative to a bread basket, but it is a practical way of helping to harmonize a table setting. Choose from a wide range of lace trims.

TECHNIQUES

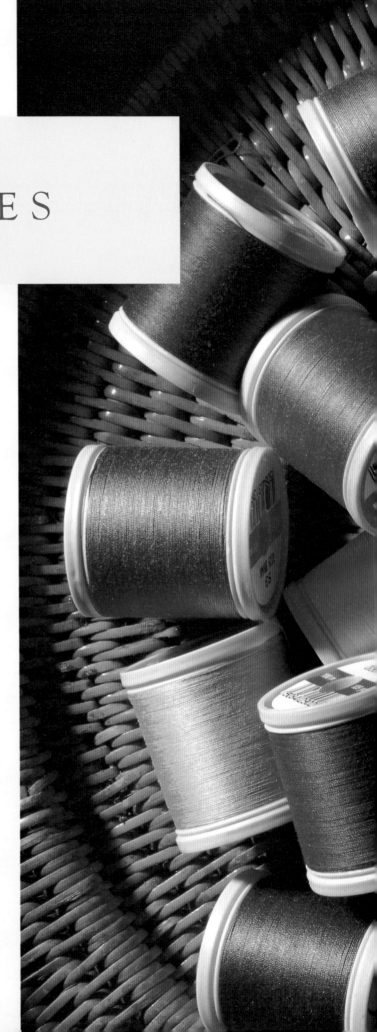

The techniques used in this book are all quite straightforward and are shown here in step-by-step detail. There is also information on equipment, how to alter curtains for windows if dimensions differ from the size for which they were originally intended, and how to enlarge and reduce patterns. When trying a sewing technique for the first time, it is advisable to have a test run on a spare piece of fabric if possible.

EQUIPMENT

WHEN ADDING to your work basket, buy the best-quality sewing equipment you feel you can afford; more expensive items usually outlast cheaper ones. Scissors are the costly items, and more than one pair is needed as different sizes are required for different tasks, but a good-quality pair should last a lifetime.

Some projects in this book require specialist items that need only be bought if necessary. But for ease of work and professional results, your sewing basket should contain the following general equipment.

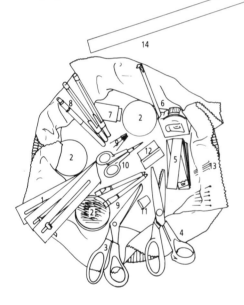

1 Sewing and knitting gauge
2 Pins
3 Cutting-out shears
4 Pinking shears (optional)
5 Tape measure
6 Decorator's steel ruler
7 Cotton
8 Fabric marking pens
9 Machine needles
10 Small scissors
11 Thimble
12 Tailor's chalk
13 Hand sewing needles
14 Yard stick

General Sewing Equipment

Dressmakers' scissors: 8 in (20 cm) or 9 in (23 cm), side-bent to give a comfortable hold, made from forged steel. They can be sharpened and adjusted.

Small scissors: which are sharp right to the point, used for snipping and trimming.

A steel tape measure: is invaluable for measuring windows for curtains, etc.

Sewing and knitting gauge: a small metal ruler with an adjustable slide measurement marker.

Medium-size scissors: 6 in (15 cm) for cutting patterns and other paper.

Tapemeasure: preferably a fiberglass one which will not stretch.

Yardstick: for marking long lines either on paper or fabric.

Tailor's chalk: a special chalk for use on fabric, available in various colors, in tablet or pencil form.

Fabric pens/pencils: for quick marking. Some fade away, others are removed by water. Always test on the fabric being used.

Pins: Dressmakers' steel pins with highly polished points will not snag fabrics. Several specialized ones are also available. Extra-fine steel pins $1\frac{3}{16}$ in (30 cm) long are recommended.

Hand sewing needles: An assorted pack gives a selection of lengths and sizes suitable for most fabrics.

Machine needles: come in a variety of types and sizes. Purchase the system that your sewing machine manual advises.

Basting cotton: is a soft thread which breaks easily, so it does not damage fabric as it is being pulled out.

Thimble: should be worn for all hand sewing, including basting; very necessary when working with thicker fabrics.

Sewing machine: gives a strong stitch that withstands the everyday wear and tear of many items. Your machine should be able to produce a straight stitch in different lengths and zigzag stitch in various widths.

PRESSING
For professional pressing the following is needed:
Steam iron (used dry)
Terrycloth towels
Cheesecloth
Ironing board: preferably with felt underlay and cotton cover.

Non-essential items
Non-essential items that are very useful when making certain projects include the following:

Bodkin: A thick, blunt, round, or flat needle with a large eye for threading elastic or tape into hems or casings.

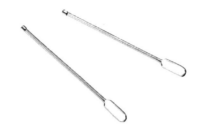

Thread snips: for cutting thread only. (Using them prevents blunting the small scissors).

Rouleau turner: A long thick needle, sometimes with a ball end, which can be pushed into a bias tube. The fabric is sewn to the eye before the turner is inserted into the tube to turn it right side out.

Overlocker/serger: machine that trims, sews and neatens in one operation very quickly.

Trimming and tape maker: A most useful, easy-to-use gadget for making your own binding. Strips of fabric, cut on the bias, are fed through the tape maker and as they are pulled through, the sides of the bias are folded, ready to be pressed with the iron.

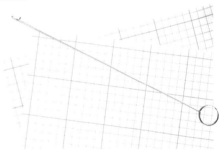

Pattern paper: is special paper printed with squares for scaling patterns on a grid system.

Flexible curve: can be shaped to follow any line.

Cutting board: Made from cardboard, it folds for easy storage and is printed with squares generally 1 in (2.5 cm). It can be used for cutting out, calculating fabric, and making patterns from a diagram.

WORKING WITH FABRIC

MOST UPHOLSTERY fabrics are made in the following widths, 48 in (122 cm), 54 in (136 cm) and 60 in (152cm) and are rolled on cardboard tubes by the manufacturer, but some, and lining materials, are folded, and then are wound onto a rectangular piece of composite board. A ticket should give the fabric content, care instructions, and where appropriate, the pattern repeat measurement.

When buying fabric it is always advisable to buy a little bit extra to allow for uneven cutting.

The descriptive terms used for fabric will soon become familiar.

- The *selvage* is the firm woven edge of fabric. It should not be used, but trimmed away.
- The *straight grain* is parallel to the selvage, and it is important that the cut ends, which are across the width of the fabric, are straightened before cutting lengths.
- The *bias* is a diagonal line across the weave of the fabric. To find the true bias; measure the same distance along the selvage and the cut edge, having first made sure the latter is at right angles to the selvage, mark the points measured, and draw a line using tailor's chalk and a yardstick.
- The *crosswise grain* runs from selvage to selvage.

Cutting fabric

▲ All fabric should be cut on the straight grain, that is, where the warp (the lengthwise thread parallel to the selvage) is at right angles to the weft (the crosswise thread). Therefore, before cutting lengths it will be necessary to straighten the cut edge. To do this, snip into the selvage and pull out a thread if the weave is loose enough; alternatively, use a try square and mark a line with tailor's chalk. Cut across the fabric on the resulting line.

- When cutting out fabric, place the left hand lightly on the fabric to the left of the pattern or marked line and the scissors held in the right hand ready to cut, having the pattern or marked line to the right of the scissors. Reverse left and right if you are left-handed.
- Cut all lengths in the same direction. With some fabrics, the direction of the design is obvious, as the word 'TOP' is actually printed on the selvage. Other fabrics, even solid ones, have to be scrutinised, as they could have a sheen which affects their appearance when viewed in different lights. Velvets, for example, can appear darker or lighter when viewed in a hanging position – when used with the pile running upward, they seem richer in color, and lighter with the pile running downward. An advantage with the latter is that the pile can be kept dust free by regular brushing.

Joining fabric

- Shades require joining with an open seam placed as unobtrusively as possible. Roman shades (above) are better made without a seam, but if it cannot be avoided, an equal amount on each side of a central panel could be added, and a flat trim machined over the seam on the right side can look attractive. Balloon shades can have a seam placed under a pleat, and festoon shades where a line of rings will be creating ruching.

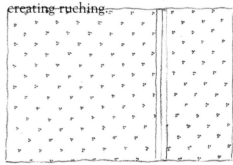

▲ When making large items, fabric has to be joined to attain the necessary width. Each curtain can require 1½/2/2½ widths, and any half width is placed to the sides farthest away from the center, where the curtains meet when closed. Unlined curtains are better joined with a run and fell seam and lined curtains with an open seam.

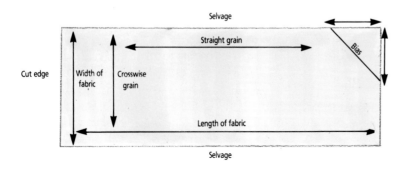

Selvage · Straight grain · Bias · Cut edge · Width of fabric · Crosswise grain · Length of fabric · Selvage

▲ Bedspreads and tablecloths (above) have an equal amount added to each side of a full width. Both can be joined with open seams and the raw edges finished.

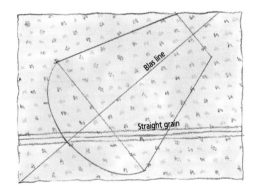

Bias line

Straight grain

▲ Extra material needed for a swag is joined on the straight grain with an open seam before the swag is cut out. The seam would be positioned in the bottom corner and would be hidden within the pleats when made.

Pinning fabric

Place pins diagonally when pinning a pattern to fabric ready for cutting out and put them well within the edges; only a few pins are necessary. The exception to this "rule" comes when working with a fabric that is easily marked by pins: place the pins within the seam allowance.

• When pinning two layers of fabric together, place pins raw edges inward to prevent pushing one layer of fabric ahead of the other. The exception to this tip is when you have piping on one layer; then the pins have to go along the seam.

Pressing fabric

• Always have the iron and ironing board ready to press at each stage, and when pressing large items, have your ironing board near a table to hold the weight of the item.

• Make sure the iron setting is right for the type of fabric, and always test-press a piece before beginning your project.

• Pressing cloths are needed, and several types are available. Cheesecloth has the added advantage that you can see through it and therefore position your iron correctly. Buy 1 yd (1 m) of cheesecloth and cut it in half to provide two pressing cloths; one to use damp and the other dry. To make a cloth damp, soak it in water and wring out firmly. This is adequate for light/medium fabrics, but fold it double for thicker materials.

• Use the iron with an up-and-down action rather than sliding it along as when ironing clothes.

• To press seams, first press along the seam with layers of fabric together as sewn and covered with a damp cloth. Then press the seam open, using your fingers and the point of the iron to open the seam. A final press with a damp cloth is required. If the fabric is thick, tuck scrap pieces of the same fabric under each side of the open seam. It is sometimes necessary to place a dry cloth over the seam and re-press.

• A seam on the edge of an item, such as the self-bordered square pillow, requires preparation before pressing. After turning right side out, roll the seam between fingers and thumbs to bring it to the edge, and baste as you go along. Press well, using a damp cloth, warm/hot iron, and medium pressure with the side of the iron just over the edge of the seam.

• There are a few fabrics that require dry pressing only. For these always place a dry pressing cloth over the fabric to prevent any damage to it and experiment with spare material if you are doubtful.

• Placing a towel on the ironing board prevents raised textured fabrics from being flattened when pressed.

• Velvet can be pressed on another piece of the same velvet placed right side up, but ideally on a needleboard.

HAND STITCHING

WHEN HAND sewing, especially on dark fabrics, work in natural light if possible, although daylight bulbs are now available and well worth purchasing. Choose matching thread suitable for the fabric for any permanent stitching, synthetic for man-made fabrics and cotton for material made from natural fibers. For temporary and marking stitches use basting thread, which is a special soft thread made for the purpose which will not damage fabric when being taken out. Do not work with a long piece of thread; the length of your arm is quite sufficient. Cutting, not breaking, the thread from the reel, makes threading a needle easier.

Needles need to be appropriate for the fabric and thread; fine needles pierce the fabric more easily, and you are less likely to snag or pull a thread in the weave. Mixed packs of needles include various sizes and lengths from which to select; find what is most comfortable for use to give a good result.

There is some hand sewing on nearly everything that is made from fabric, possibly only basting, which is merely a temporary stitch until a permanent machine stitch has been worked. Hand sewing of curtain hems is, in most cases, preferable, as the stitches are worked so that they are invisible from the right side. When sewing hems, have the bulk of the curtain on a table with the hem toward you; this way, the weight is supported, and the curtain will not get so creased.

A thimble should be worn on the middle finger of your sewing hand for protection, especially when sewing thicker or firmly woven materials.

Basting

A temporary stitch used to hold two pieces of fabric together while further processes are worked. The length of the stitches needs to be made in relation to the fabric; fine material would require a smaller stitch, while for a fabric that is thicker, and unlikely to slip, a larger stitch would be adequate. If you find you have pulled the stitches too tightly, do not rebaste. Just snip the thread to release the tension every now and then along the length of the seam before stitching. Always remove pins as you baste.

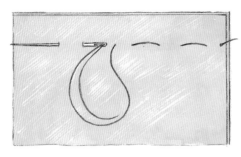

Using basting thread, knot one end to secure the thread in the material when making the first stitch. Do not work more than two stitches at a time before pulling the needle through, and do *not* pull the thread tightly; otherwise, the fabric will pucker. To finish, fasten the thread with a backstitch and cut it off, leaving a 2 in (5 cm) end.

Tailor's tacks

Tailor's tacks are worked using double basting thread without a knot on the end and are used to mark a certain point for matching up with another piece of fabric.

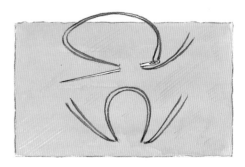

Make a stitch $\frac{1}{4}$ in (6 mm) and leave the ends $\frac{3}{8}$ in (1 cm); make another stitch over the first, leaving a loop $\frac{3}{4}$ in (2 cm); repeat to make a second loop and cut the thread, leaving the ends $\frac{3}{8}$ in (1 cm).

Backstitch

A secure stitch used for short runs and worked from right to left. Use thread with a knot on the end.

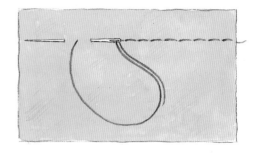

Bring the needle up through the fabric from the back, a little way from the beginning to allow the needle to be placed back at the beginning and down through the fabric. Then the needle is brought up ahead of the first stitch. Continue in this way until the end, when two backstitches are worked on the spot.

Ladder stitch

Ladder stitch (sometimes called sliptacking) is also a basting stitch. It is used when matching a pattern in joining two pieces of material and it is worked from the right side.

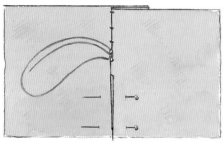

Press the seam allowance under on one side, taking care not to stretch the fabric. Place the folded edge over the seam allowance, matching the pattern exactly, and pin firmly in place. Knot the thread under the folded edge and bring the needle up to the right side. Move the needle across the fold and take a stitch in line with the folded edge. Pull through and take a stitch across the folded edge again, between the two layers of fabric. Take a stitch of ¾ in (2 cm) and bring the needle back through to the right side.

Blanket stitch

Blanket stitch can be used to finish raw edges securely or attach curtain rings, to a tieback for example.

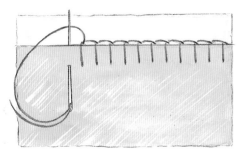

Fasten the thread under the raw edge of the fabric and bring the needle through to the right side. With the needle held at a right angle, loop the thread behind the point. Pull through and continue with even stitches and the thread loops lying neatly along the edge.

Slipstitch

A stitch that is very nearly invisible on both sides of the fabric when used on a hemline or any other folded edge.

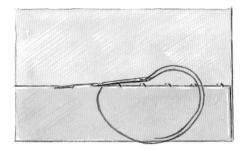

Secure the end of the thread with a couple of stitches inside the folded edge, then slide the needle along the fold of the hem for ¼ in (5 mm) and pull through. With the point of the needle, pick up a few threads from the fabric exactly opposite, pull through and insert into the fold again. Continue in this way, taking care not to pull the thread too tightly. When using this stitch for mitered corners, slide the needle along both folds, first on one side and then the other.

Catchstitch

A stitch to join two layers of fabric loosely together, worked slightly under one fabric, making an invisible join. This is an ideal stitch to attach a detachable lining to a curtain.

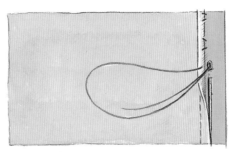

Fold back the lining and take a small stitch in the side hem, then a stitch in the curtain. Work further stitches first on one side, then the other. Do not pull the thread tightly.

Lockstitch

Lockstitch is used in curtain-making to anchor lining and interlining to curtain fabric. It is worked with the fabric and lining placed with wrong sides together.

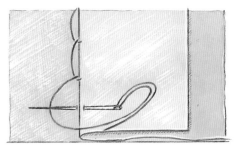

Pin the centers together down the complete length and fold the lining back. Make two or three stitches in the fold of the lining near the top. Then, working downward and keeping the thread loose, pick up a couple of threads from the fabric and the lining. The needle goes over the thread to "lock" it, and the stitches need to be approximately 4–6 in (10–15 cm) apart.

Herringbone stitch

Herringbone stitch is worked from left to right and is a securing stitch. The stitches should not be worked too tightly, as this allows them to be seen from the right side.

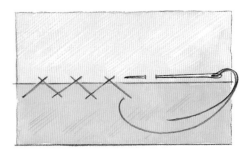

Fasten the thread with a couple of stitches and bring the needle up through the hem. Move it diagonally to the right just above the hem, and pick up a few threads from the fabric. With the needle moved farther to the right, take a stitch in the hem. The needle is held horizontal throughout and the thread is kept below it.

MACHINE STITCHING

MACHINE SEWING produces a strong permanent stitch that will withstand the test of time and the use of the item. An instruction book comes with every sewing machine and should be studied for the various features and explanations on the tension and setting of the length for straight stitch, width for zigzag stitch, etc.

Always test the stitch on a doubled spare piece of the fabric to be used for a project, selecting the needle, thread, and stitch length that are appropriate.

Remember to change the needle frequently, after about eight to twelve hours' sewing, and make sure you are using the correct type and size for the fabric and thread. Failing to do this will result in missed and badly formed stitches.

If your sewing machine does not seem to be sewing correctly, first change the needle. If there is no improvement, check the threading of both the top and bottom. The bobbin thread has to wind off in a certain way – clockwise or counter-clockwise – your instruction book should make it clear.

If the table you are using for machine sewing is not large enough to hold the material, place an adjustable ironing board at table height to the left of the table and use it to support the material. Alternatively, place three or four chairs with their backs against the table and drape the material over the chair backs with the material resting on the seats.

If you are stitching with the seam just pinned, always remove the pins as you work.

Using a machine

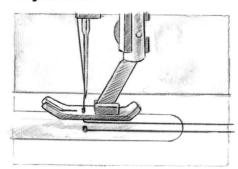

1 When starting to machine stitch, hold the top and bottom threads together toward the back to prevent them from tangling underneath.

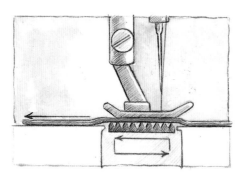

2 Your machine will feed the material under the pressure foot, without any need to push it from the front or pull it from the back. If you do either, stitching will be uneven. Light fingertip control to guide the fabric on the stitching line is all that is required.

Straight stitch

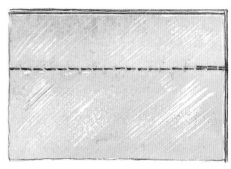

This stitch is used in varying lengths and needs to be adjusted for different fabrics; the stitch is equally strong whether small or large. It is the stitch most used for seams. Always make the first test run with a medium-length stitch setting on a double layer of material.

Edge stitch

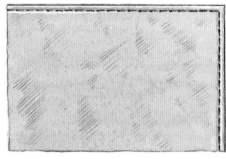

A straight stitch worked on the right side very near to the edge of the fabric.

Top stitch

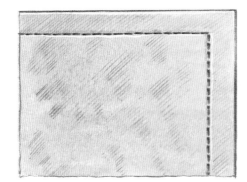

A straight stitch worked with the right side of the fabric up normally $\frac{1}{4}$ in (6 mm) from the edge unless a specific measurement is given.

Zigzag stitch

This is used for finishing seams and is ideal on frequently laundered items such as bed linen. Trimmings such as ribbon and flat braid look better when sewn on with zigzag stitch. Use it also to sew touch-and-close fastener tape in place.

Gathering stitch

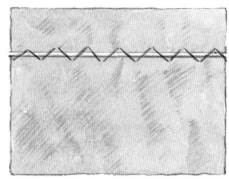

Gathering on medium and thick materials can be made easier by machining over a thin cord with zigzag stitch.

OVERLOCKING

An overlocker/serger trims, sews, and finishes a seam in one operation at twice the speed of a conventional sewing machine. A three-thread stitch using one upper sewing thread, in either the left or the right needle (it depends on the fabric being sewn) and two loopers threaded with overlocking thread is ideal for finishing seams. A four-thread stitch; two upper sewing threads and two loopers threaded with overlocking thread, produces a strong seam suitable for bed linen items.

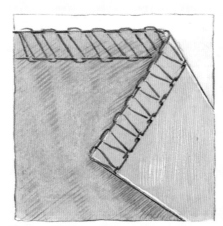

Three-thread stitch

Four-thread stitch

Gathering stitch

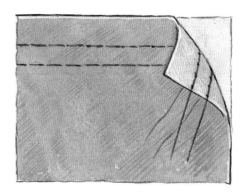

Set the machine to the longest straight stitch setting and reduce the top tension a little. Make a test run with a single or double layer of fabric, whichever is being used in the project. With the right side up, work two rows of stitching, one just within the seam allowance and the other $\frac{1}{4}$ in (6 mm) from the first. Pull the bobbin threads together to form the gathers, distributing them evenly. If a long length of fabric needs to be gathered, divide the length in equal sections and break the thread between each.

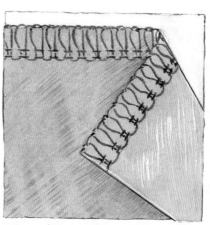

SEAMS

THERE ARE many different ways of joining seams, and it is essential to sew the seam that is appropriate for the fabric and the item you are making. A plain, open seam is used for joining two pieces of fabric together. A double seam or French seam is used to enclose raw edges, especially on lightweight or sheer fabrics; it is a very hard-wearing seam. The run-and-fell seam, also a strong seam, gives a flatter finish than a French seam and is ideal for items that require frequent washing. Run-and-fell seams are suitable for unlined items such as kitchen or bathroom curtains. A flat, lapped seam is used to join interlining.

Open seam

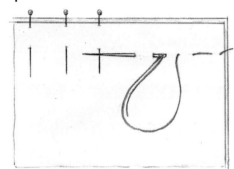

1 Place the pieces of fabric right sides together and pin at right angles from the raw edges inward. Baste just inside the seam line and remove pins.

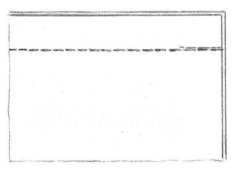

2 Machine stitch, using the normal seam allowance of ⅝ in (1.5 cm) unless otherwise stated. Work down the length of the item, i.e., from the top of a curtain toward the hemline, and reverse the stitching for a short way at each end to secure the ends. Remove the basting.

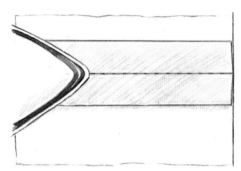

3 Press the stitching into the fabric first, then open the seam flat and press the seam.

Lapped seam

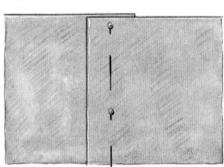

1 With the right side of both pieces of fabric uppermost, overlap one piece over the other by ⅝ in (1.5 cm).

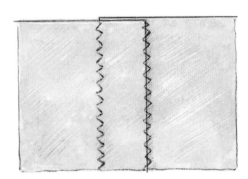

2 Machine stitch with a large zigzag stitch to secure the raw edges, or sew by hand using herringbone stitch.

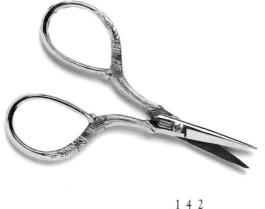

French seam

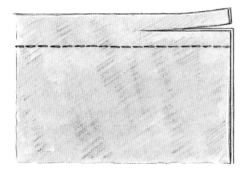

❶ Place the pieces of the fabric wrong sides together and pin from the raw edges inward. Baste just inside the seam line, if necessary. Machine stitch $\frac{3}{8}$ in (9 mm) from the raw edges, and then trim the seam to $\frac{1}{8}$ in (3 mm). Remove the basting.

❷ Turn the fabric so that the right sides are together. Roll the seam between fingers and thumbs to bring it to the edge. If you moisten your fingers, it will help you to grip the fabric. Baste as you work along the seam, enclosing the raw edge of the first seam.

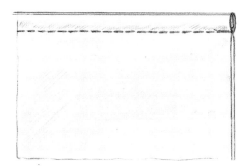

❸ Press the seam. Then machine stitch $\frac{1}{4}$ in (6 mm) from the edge of the item, and press the seam again.

Run and fell seam

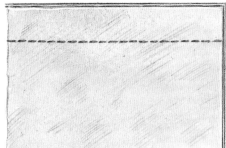

❶ Place the pieces of fabric wrong sides together and pin. Baste the seam and then machine stitch $\frac{5}{8}$ in (1.5 cm) from the raw edges. If you are using a thick fabric, make the seam wider, having allowed for this when cutting out.

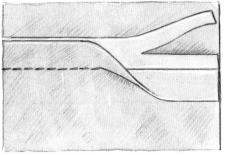

❷ Press the seam open. Trim one side of the seam allowance only, down to $\frac{1}{4}$ in (6 mm).

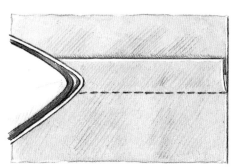

❸ Press the seam to one side with the larger seam allowance on top.

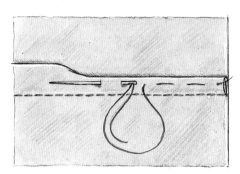

❹ Turn the larger seam allowance under $\frac{1}{4}$ in (6 mm), basting it down as you work along the seam.

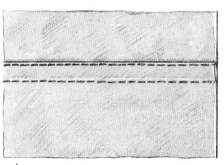

❺ Press the seam before and after machine stitching it to the fabric close to the edge. Do not press terrycloth.

MITERED CORNERS

A MITERED CORNER gives a neat, flat appearance to the hems of curtains or table linen. How you make a miter depends on what it is for. To make a miter with the same turning on both sides of the corner, as for a tablecloth, use Method One. To make a miter with a single-turn side and a double-turn bottom hem, as for tube-lined and locked-in lined curtains, use Method Two. For single-turn side and bottom hems, for interlined and lined curtains, use Method Three.

Method One

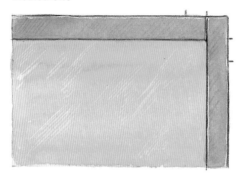

❶ Turn under 1 in (2.5 cm) on both sides of the corner and press in place.

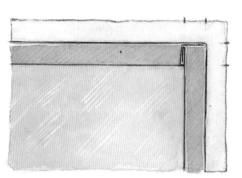

❷ Make a second turn of 1 in (2.5 cm) on both sides and press again.

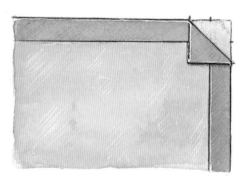

❸ Unfold the second turn and fold in the corner on the diagonal. Press the diagonal fold.

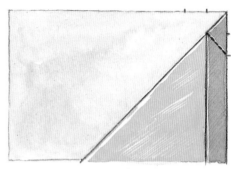

❹ Unfold the diagonal and place the right sides of the fabric together. Machine stitch along the creaseline of the diagonal fold.

❺ Trim the seam to $\frac{1}{4}$ in (6 mm) and press it open.

❻ Turn the corner right side out. Re-fold the hem and machine stitch in place.

Method Two

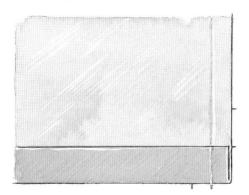

1 Press the single-turn side hem and the double-turn bottom hem. Unfold the side and the second turn of the bottom hem.

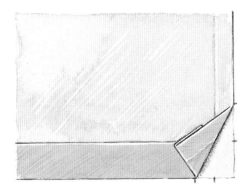

2 Press a diagonal fold, having twice the allowance of the side measurement along the bottom, and twice the allowance of the hem measurement along the side.

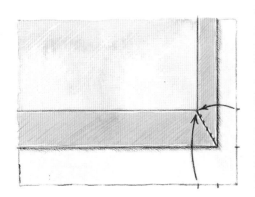

3 Refold and slipstitch in place. If the fabric is very thick, trim off the excess before refolding.

Method Three

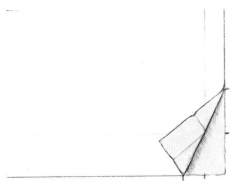

1 Press the single-turn side hem and the single-turn bottom hem. Unfold the side and bottom hems. Proceed as steps 1 and 2, Method Two.

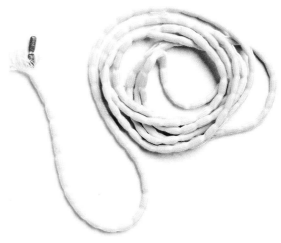

WEIGHTS

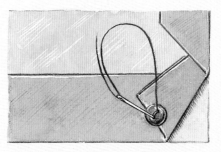

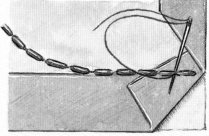

The addition of coin weights significantly improves the hanging of curtains, and they can be added while mitering the corners. They should be sewn to the hem before stitching the miter. Alternatively, lead-weight tape available by the yard can be slotted along the full length of the hem. This needs catching in at each end and in several places along the hemline.

FASTENERS

MANY furnishing items, such as pillow and duvet covers, can be fastened in different ways. Zippers are neat and strong, and are ideal on cushions, especially seat cushions. Touch-and-close fastener tape is very versatile, and there are two types that can be used when making furnishings; one is sewn to both sections, the other is a very efficient way of attaching valances or shades to a valance board/shelf. The self-adhesive hook side is pressed into position on the board/shelf, and the loop side sewn in place to the valance or shade.

Fabric ties are another form of fastening, which add that personal touch and give a completely coordinated look. The length and width of a self-fabric tie depends on whether a simple knot or a bow is required and if the function is to pull two edges together, or if a pillow needs to be held in place by being tied to the back of the chair. It is a simple matter to position and pin a length of tape in place, tie a bow and then take a measurement. The finished width of the tie can be very narrow, ¾ in (2 cm), medium 2 in (5 cm) or 4 in (10 cm) wide, or even wider.

Fabric ties

1 Cut two strips of fabric on the straight grain, double the finished width plus ¾ in (2 cm) seam allowance by the length required.

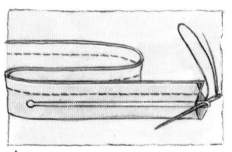

2 Fold in half lengthwise, pin and machine stitch with a ⅜ in (1 cm) seam, removing the pins as you work. Push a large-eyed, long, blunt needle or bodkin into the tube and firmly stitch to one side of the tube.

3 Turn the strip right side out by working the needle/bodkin down the tube, ruching the fabric over, then easing it off until the strip is completely turned. Press well and finish one end by hand. Insert the raw edge in a seam or turn the raw edge under and stitch in place.

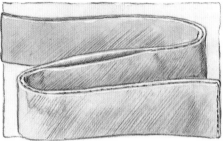

4 For a wider tie, leave a central opening on the long edge to enable the ends to be machine stitched. Turn right side out through the opening.

Touch-and-close

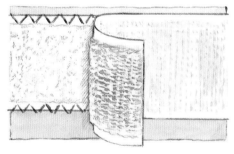

Touch-and-close consists of two pieces of tape-like material woven from nylon, one side having tiny soft loops and the other tiny firm hooks. Press them together and they make a very strong bond. Pull them apart to sew them in place with zigzag stitch, aligning one with the other to guarantee they meet correctly for fastening.

Touch-and-close dots are small disks of the same type of material and are held in place with a triangle of hand or machine stitching.

Zippers

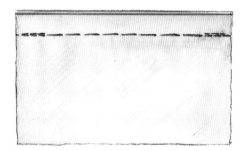

1 With the right sides of the fabric together, machine stitch the full length of the seam as follows: stitch the seams up to the zipper opening with a normal-size stitch, and reverse to secure the stitching. Then stitch the placket with the largest size stitch. Press the seam open.

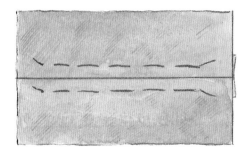

2 Baste guide lines on the right side of the fabric $\frac{1}{4}$ in (6 mm) on both sides of the seam where the zipper is to be positioned.

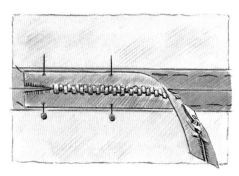

3 Position the closed zipper, right side down, on the wrong side of the fabric over the seam line, centering the teeth. Pin to hold it while you baste it in place from the right side. Thread two needles with basting thread and baste along the two sides of the zipper alternately.

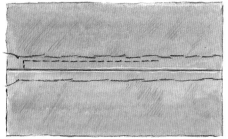

4 Fit the zipper foot to the machine and stitch the zipper in place on the right side. Start at the seam at the bottom of the zipper and stitch across at a right angle to the zipper, pivoting the fabric around the needle when you reach the guide line. Continue stitching, pausing with the needle in the fabric 3 in (7.5 cm) from the zipper tab end.

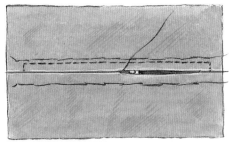

5 Release the zipper foot and carefully take out some of the long machine stitches to open the zipper past the machine needle. Lower the presser foot and continue sewing to the end of the guide line. Pivot the fabric around the needle with the needle in the fabric and stitch to the seam line.

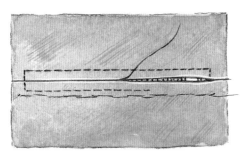

6 Machine stitch the other side of the zipper in the same way. Be careful to stitch a straight line past the zipper tab.

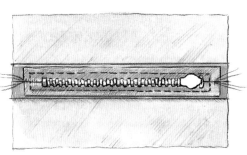

7 Remove the basting and remaining long machine stitches. Knot the machine threads on the wrong side.

Grippers

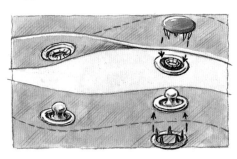

A practical and decorative non-sew fastener with two parts to each section that fasten in place on each side of the fabric. They are sold in packs with full instructions and a hand tool to hold them in position until they are attached.

Gripper tape

Gripper tape consists of two pieces of tape with snaps or grippers attached at intervals along the length. Tapes are sewn on separately with a straight stitch using the zipper foot.

BINDING AND PIPING

BINDING RAW edges gives a quick, neat finish. Use bias binding for a shaped item as it will go around corners easily since it has a certain amount of stretch. Straight binding is needed when a firm edge is required, as for the swag and tails.

Piping gives a finishing touch to a pillow and can be made in a contrasting or coordinating color to add interest. It also gives extra strength to seat cushions or anything that will be in constant use. Cording is made from strips of material cut on the bias with a piping cord inserted. Piping cord is made in different numbered sizes, with 3–5 being the most often used on furnishing and accessories. Always check that it is preshrunk.

QUICK BIAS BINDING
There is now a useful gadget on the market which forms folded edges on the side of the bias strip (see page 134). The bias strip is fed through a wide end and pulled through a narrow one to turn the edges, which are pressed with an iron as they appear.

Continuous bias binding

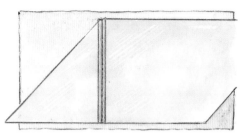

1 Mark the bias at one side of the piece of fabric and cut off the end corner.

Move the triangular scrap of fabric to the other side of the rectangle, and with right sides together, join them with a $\frac{1}{4}$ in (6 mm) open seam. Press the seam open.

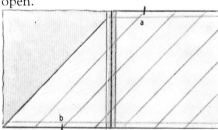

2 On the wrong side of the piece of fabric, mark cutting lines to the required width parallel to the ends. Mark a $\frac{1}{4}$ in (6 mm) seam allowance at the sides. Mark with pins points A and B on the seamline as shown.

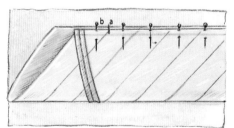

3 With the right sides facing, bring together the two pins at points A and B. Pin the sides together along the seamline to produce a tube with the width of a single strip protruding at each end of the seam.

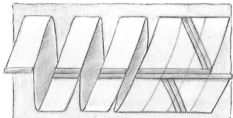

4 Baste along the line of pins, and remove the pins. Machine stitch along the seam line, and press the seam open carefully. Cut along the marked lines to make one continuous strip of bias binding.

Applying a bias strip

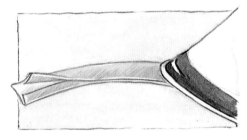

1 Fold and press the binding in half. Holding the bias binding in the left hand, curve the binding to fit the item using a medium hot iron.

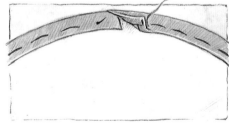

2 Insert the edges of the item between the folded bias binding. Pin, baste and zigzag in place, finish the join of the binding by turning under one edge to overlap the other.

Straight binding

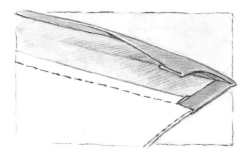

This is a strip of fabric preferably cut on the straight lengthwise grain of material, but can be cut from the width of material on the crossways grain. Measurements for cutting the strips and applying them are given in the instructions for the individual items.

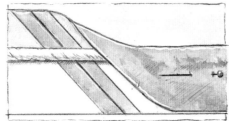

3 Lay the piping cord along the center of the strip of fabric on the wrong side. Fold the fabric over the piping cord. Align the raw edges and pin the fabric near the cord. Baste along the line of pins, and remove the pins. With the zipper foot on the machine, stitch close to the cord. Remove basting.

3 Cut across the cording on one end. On the other end, pull back the bias strip and cut the cord only, making sure that the ends butt together snugly. Turn the bias strip under across the free end to finish it and cover the raw edge of the first end. Finish stitching the cording on the seam line.

To make cording

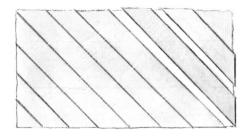

1 Cut bias strips from the fabric $1\frac{1}{2}$–$2\frac{3}{8}$ in (4–6 mm) wide, depending on the size of the cord. The strips should be wide enough to go around the cord and have a double seam allowance of $\frac{5}{8}$ in (1.5 cm).

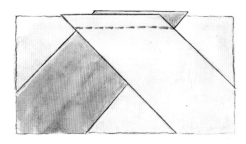

2 Join the strips of fabric on the straight grain with $\frac{1}{4}$ in (6 mm) open seams, and press the seams open.

To apply cording

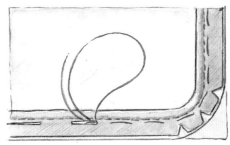

1 Place the cording to the right side of the first fabric piece. Align the raw edges and pin the cording to the fabric piece. Baste them together, snipping the curves or corners as you work, and leave an overlap of 1 in (2.5 cm) where the ends of the cording meet. Remove the pins.

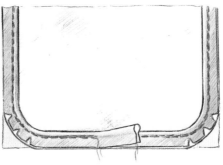

2 Machine stitch the cording in place, starting 1 in (2.5 cm) from one end and stopping the same distance from the other end.

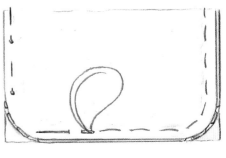

4 Place the first and second pieces of fabric right sides together. Pin and baste them together, and remove the pins. Turn the work over so that you can follow the first line of stitching from applying the piping, and stitch the seam, using the zipper foot.

RUFFLES AND PLEATS

RUFFLES MADE from single and double fabric can be used to add an attractive trimming. Made in a contrasting color, they will give an added interest to many home furnishings and are an excellent way to coordinate the item with other focal points in a room.

A pleated trim can be used instead of a gathered ruffle. It is especially attractive at the bottom of a tieback. The fabric required for a pleated trim is three times the measurement to be trimmed. Experiment with the fabric that is going to be used; smaller pleats can be formed on thin/medium materials, but thicker fabric will require larger pleats.

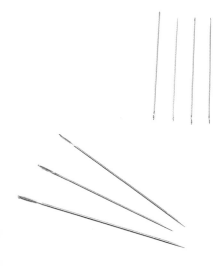

Single ruffle

A single ruffle can be any width that is in proportion with the item. The length of the piece of fabric should be at least $1\frac{1}{2}$ times the measurement around the item, such as a pillowcase, to which it will be added.

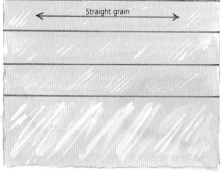

1 Cut out strips of fabric on the straight grain. Remember to add on a $\frac{5}{8}$ in (1.5 cm) seam allowance and a double hem allowance of $\frac{3}{8}-\frac{3}{4}$ cm (1 to 2 cm), depending on the thickness of the fabric.

2 Join the strips of fabric with run-and-fell seams into one continuous round. Turn up $\frac{1}{4}$ in (6 mm) twice to the wrong side all round the bottom edge of the ruffle and pin. Baste the hem and remove the pins. Machine stitch the hem.

3 Divide the ruffle into four sections and mark with pins. Machine stitch two rows of gathering, with the first row just inside the seam allowance and the other $\frac{1}{4}$ in (6 mm) above it. Break off the threads at each pin.

4 Divide the item to be trimmed into four sections and mark with pins. Pull up the bobbin threads on each section of the ruffle so that the sections match those on the item being trimmed.

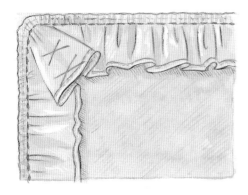

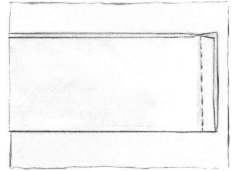

Round double ruffle

If the fabric for the ruffle is used double, the need for a hem is eliminated. To make a double ruffle, you will need twice the finished width of the ruffle plus a double seam allowance. For a finished 2 in (5 cm) ruffle with a seam allowance of $\frac{1}{2}$ in (1.3 cm), cut strips on the straight grain 5 in (12.5 cm) wide by the length required.

5 With right sides together, place the ruffle on the item being trimmed, matching the division marks and aligning the raw edges. Adjust the gathers evenly and pin the ruffle in place. Baste the ruffle in place and remove the pins. Machine stitch.

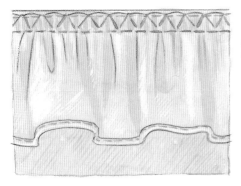

6 Machine stitch again $\frac{1}{4}$ in (6 mm) above the first line of stitching. Trim the seam close to the stitching, and zigzag stitch along the seam to finish it.

2 Join the strips with an open seam and press. Fold in half lengthwise, right sides together, and stitch the ends.

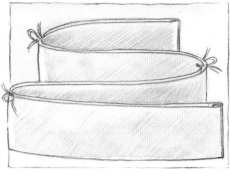

3 Turn right side out and press. Divide into four and mark with tailor's tacks.

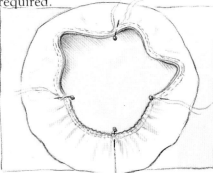

▲ Join the strips into a round with open seams, and press the seams open. Fold the fabric in half lengthwise with the wrong sides together and then proceed as for the single ruffle.

Straight double ruffle

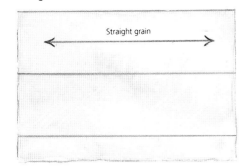

Straight grain

1 Cut strips $7\frac{1}{4}$ in (18 cm) wide by twice the bottom measurement of the item being trimmed, allowing extra for any seams that are necessary to make the required length.

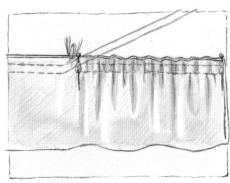

4 Run two rows of gathering stitch, breaking the threads at the tailor's tacks. The ruffle is now ready to apply.

Pleats

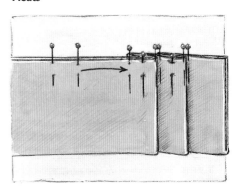

For $\frac{1}{2}$ in (1.3 cm) pleats mark the raw edge with pins $\frac{1}{2}$ in (1.3 cm)– 1 in (2.5 cm) apart all the way along. Follow the direction of the arrows on the illustration to form the pleats.

ADAPTING CURTAINS

THE PROVISION OF SETS of curtains for all the rooms in a new house can be a daunting task – and expensive. It may be possible to adapt existing curtains to fit the new window sizes. If the curtains are too long, the quickest and easiest way to alter the length is from the top. Curtains can be lengthened by adding a contrasting or coordinating fabric to the bottom of the curtain or as a band a little way up from the bottom. Patterned fabric could be used for the insertion for a solid curtain, or vice versa, with each seam trimmed with a harmonizing braid or ribbon. You could add a ruffle at the bottom of the curtain made from the same fabric as the insertion.

If you have a pair of curtains that don't go with a window, you could make it into a decorative rod-pocket curtain, perhaps as a wall hanging or a dress curtain for an archway, using an attractive rod or pole.

Shortening curtains

Baste the lining to the curtain fabric below the heading tape, and then cut off the tape. Measure for the new length from the hemline up, trimming away any excess material from the top. Purchase new heading tape and apply it following the instructions on page 52.

Lengthening curtains

Purchase enough fabric for the depth of the insertion to give you the required curtain length. Allow extra for the seams top and bottom.

1 Undo the lining up the sides of the curtain to just above the proposed cutting line and cut across the curtain.

A quick and easy way to lengthen curtains is to add a plain or contrasting strip to the bottom of the curtain. If possible, use this strip to help co-ordinate the curtain with other furnishings in the room.

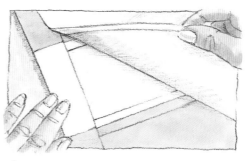

2 Place the bottom piece of the curtain and the insertion fabric right sides together with the cut edges aligned. Pin and baste together. Remove the pins and machine stitch. Place the top piece of the curtain to the other cut edge of the insertion, pin, baste and machine stitch as before. Press the seams open.

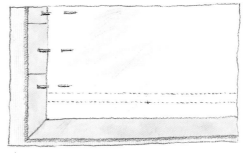

3 Lengthen the lining by adding a new piece of lining of the required depth to the bottom of the original lining.

Turn up the bottom of the lining by 1 in (2.5 cm) twice and pin it in place. Baste the hem and remove the pins. Machine stitch the hem, press it, and re-sew the lining to the sides of the curtain.

LOOP HEADINGS

Rod-pocket curtains

Cut off the curtain heading, remembering to baste the curtain and lining together just below the cutting line first.

Form a slot heading by making a double turn hem of 4 in (10 cm), pin and baste, removing the pins as you work.

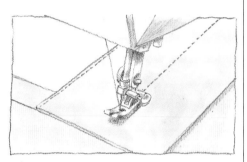

1 Machine stitch the hem and work a further row of machining 2 in (5 cm) from the first.

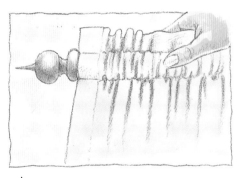

2 Push the rod or pole into the casing formed by the two rows of machining and even out the fullness. For a dress curtain make a tie-back to loop the fullness back.

FOR CURTAINS THAT remain permanently in place, without needing to be closed, a looped heading is particularly easy to make. It can be used for café curtains and is useful for attaching back-rest pillows or bedheads to a pole or rod.

For the length of each loop, measure the circumference of the pole and add 3 in (7.5 cm). For the width, the tab should be between 2 and 3 in (5 and 7.5 cm). The number of tabs will depend on the length of the pole and the width of the curtain, but, as a guide, you will need one at each end, with the remainder spaced at approximately 4 to 6 in (10 to 15 cm) intervals.

- Cut a strip of fabric long enough to cut into equal tab lengths times the width of one tab plus a $1\frac{1}{2}$ in (4 cm) seam allowance. Fold the strip in half lengthwise, with right sides facing, and stitch the long cut edge. Trim the seam and turn right side out. Press.

- Cut the required number of tabs from the joined strip of fabric, fold each one in half, then pin and baste to the top of the curtain on the right side, with the raw edges even, and the tabs spaced evenly apart.

- To make a facing, cut a $2\frac{1}{2}$ in (6.5 cm) wide strip of fabric the same width as the curtain and finish the side and bottom edges. With right sides together, pin and stitch the facing to the curtain top, turn it over to the wrong side and topstitch close to the edge to hold the tabs firmly in place.

Loop headings are very eye-catching – for dress curtains attached to an ornamental rod and café curtains. Fringing and other trimmings add visual impact.

PATTERNS AND TEMPLATES

ANY PATTERN THAT is drawn on a grid in a book or magazine needs to be scaled up to full size before using. Squared pattern paper is available which is usually printed with dark lines denoting 1 in (2.5 cm) squares, with lighter lines dividing these into $\frac{1}{2}$ in (1.25 cm) squares. If the diagram gives only half the pattern, follow it precisely as it can be used as a template and placed on a folded piece of paper to cut out as a full pattern.

Enlarging and reducing a pattern

• Count the number of squares across the top of the diagram and down one side. Count the same on the pattern paper. Number the squares along the top from left to right and down the side from top to bottom.

• Place dots where the outline of the shape intersects a grid line on the printed squares.

• When all the dots have been marked, join them to make the shape. First join any straight lines using a ruler and pencil; for curved lines, join the dots following the shape using a Flexible Curve.

• Cut out the pattern and mark any instructions printed on the grid diagram, including the seam allowance that will be required when making the item.

• As an alternative to using squared pattern paper, use a tracing or plain pattern paper placed over a cutting board. The printed grid on the board can be seen through either of these papers. When using this method, prevent the paper from moving by placing weights such as books, scissors, etc., at the corners of the paper DO NOT PIN IN PLACE.

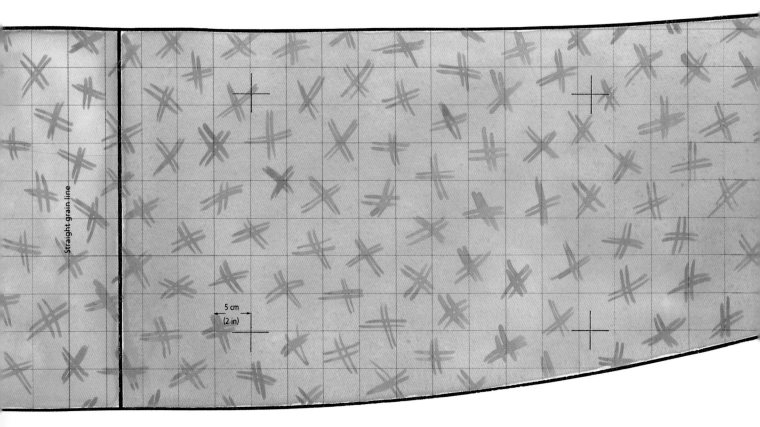

Straight grain line

5 cm
(2 in)

Making a round pattern

• To make a round pattern, you will need a square piece of paper the same size as the diameter of the finished item. Fold the piece of paper into four. With a pencil tied to a piece of string, and using one side of the square as the radius, pin the string to the folded point and draw an arc. Cut out the paper circle. For a back piece with a zipper, as in the piped round pillow, cut a second circle the same size as the first and cut the second one in half where the zipper is going to be.

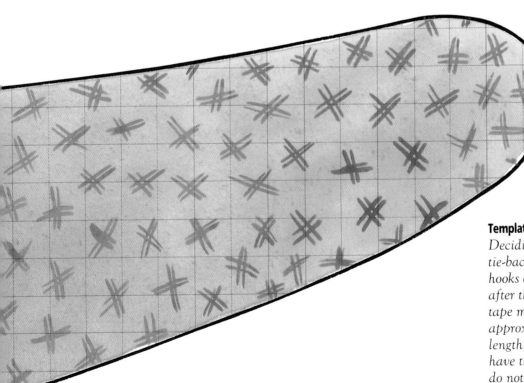

Template for tie-back

Deciding on the measurement for the tie-backs, and the positioning of the hooks on which to hang them, is taken after the curtains are hung. Hold a tape measure round the curtain approximately two-thirds down the length, adjusting the tape until you have the effect you want. The curtains do not want to be held too tightly. Mark the position for the hook which should be placed just behind the side edge of the curtain, and note the length required for the tie-back, adding $1\frac{1}{2}$ in (4 cm) to this measurement for the position of the rings.

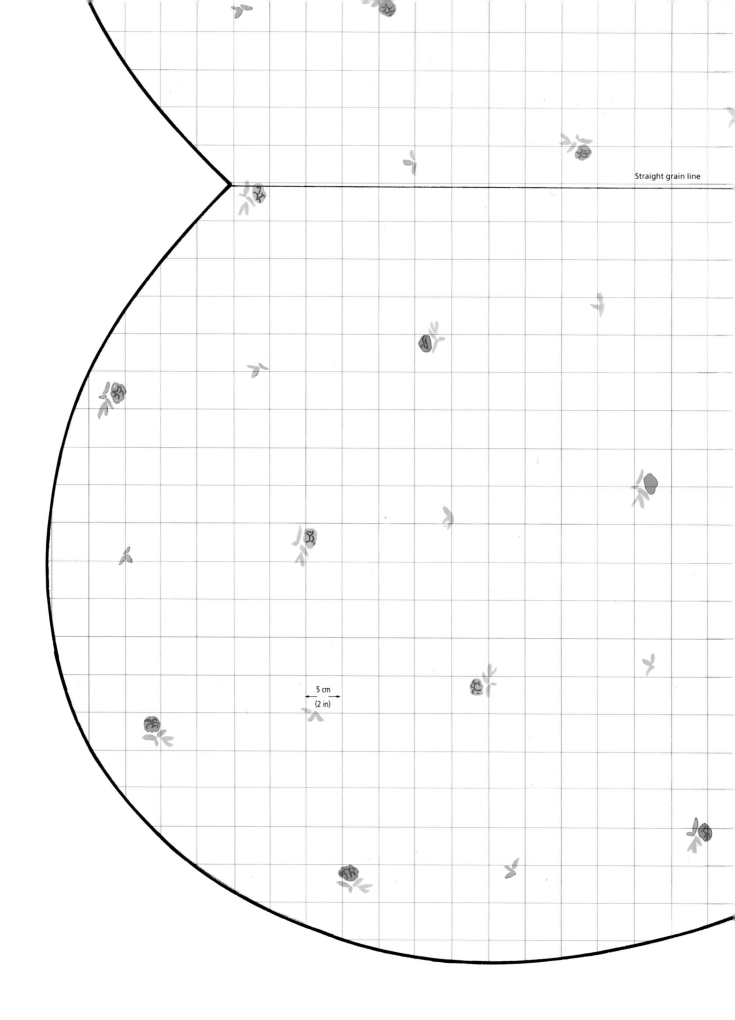

Straight grain line

5 cm
(2 in)

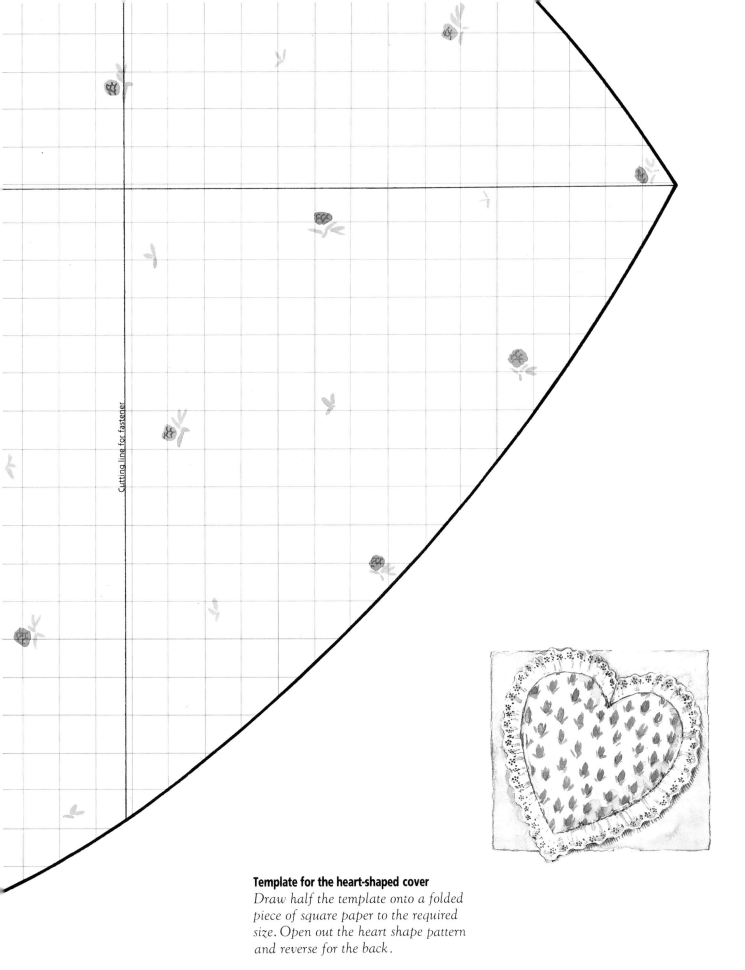

Cutting line for fastener

Template for the heart-shaped cover
Draw half the template onto a folded piece of square paper to the required size. Open out the heart shape pattern and reverse for the back.

INDEX

ACKNOWLEDGMENTS

Quarto would like to thank the following for providing photographs and transparencies, and for permission to reproduce copyright material. While every effort has been made to trace and acknowledge all copyright holders, we would like to apologize should there have been any omissions.

T = top B = bottom L = left R = right TL = top left ML = middle left BL = below left BR = below right MR = middle right

page 2	T	Alexandra Stephenson
page 2	M	Jane Churchill Ltd
page 2	B	fabric: Laura Ashley
page 2 & 3		Calico Lion
page 8		Anna French Ltd
page 9		Laura Ashley
page 10	T	Laura Ashley
page 10	B	Anna French Ltd
page 11		Arthur Sanderson and Sons Ltd
page 12	T	Anna French Ltd
page 12	B	fabric designed by Collier Campbell and distributed by Christian Fischbacher
page 14		Anna French Ltd
page 15	L	Today Interiors
page 15	R	Anna French Ltd
page 16	L	Swish Products Ltd
page 16	R	Rufflette Ltd
page 17		Zoffany
page 18		Anna French Ltd
page 19		Boras Cotton (UK) Ltd
page 20	L	Anna French Ltd
page 20	R	Boras Cotton (UK) Ltd
page 21	L	Rufflette Ltd
page 21	R	Arthur Sanderson and Son Ltd
page 22		Anna French Ltd
page 23		Boras Cotton (UK) Ltd
page 24		Anna French Ltd
page 25		Skopos Design Ltd
page 26		Arthur Sanderson and Son Ltd
page 27	TL	Jane Churchill Ltd
page 27	ML	Jane Churchill Ltd
page 27	BL	Wendy A Cushing
page 27	BR	Skopos Design Ltd
page 27	MR	Anna French Ltd
page 32		Osborne & Little
page 33	L	Laura Ashley
page 33	R	Anna French Ltd
page 34		Boras Cotton (UK) Ltd
page 36		Wesley-Barrell
page 38		Hill & Knowles Ltd
page 39		Rufflette Ltd
page 40		Byron & Byron Ltd
page 43	L	Swish Products Ltd
page 43	R	Osborne & Little
page 45		Osborne & Little
page 47	T	Laura Ashley
page 47	B	Colour Counsellors
page 48		Kirsch/Integra
page 51		Crowson Fabrics
page 53	T	Acrimo/Ibis, Sheffield
page 53	B	Boras Cotton (UK) Ltd/ Stromma

Author's acknowledgements
My sincere thanks to Barbara Carpenter and Mary Straka for their much appreciated practical help with the typing and reading the text.

I thank the following for supplying fabrics to make the step-by-step samples for the projects to be illustrated: Anna French, Monkwell Ltd and Arthur Sanderson & Sons Ltd, and Bernette for allowing the overlocker/serger stitch reference to be used.

I also thank the following suppliers: Cope and Timmins Ltd (curtain accessories); Newey Goodman Ltd (sewing accessories); C & M Offray and Son Ltd (ribbons); Perivale-Güterman (sewing thread); Rufflette Ltd (curtain heading tapes); Selectus Ltd (Hook and Loop Fastener tape); Vilene Retail (interfacing).